Love is the most important word in the English language—and the most confusing word. We use the word love in a thousand ways. However, if you are interested in the kind of love that enhances relationships and endures, *Love Like You Mean It* is for you.

Gary D. Chapman, PhD, author of *The 5 Love Languages*

Today, the word *love* is the headliner on every daytime talk show and magazine cover on the check-out stand. And sadly, Christian couples can't help but be influenced by such constant culture-speak. You see it in how edgy and uneasy we are within our relationships. Do we even recall what love looks like, sounds like, and how it acts itself out in marriage? My good friend Bob Lepine is the best guide I know for giving seasoned, practical advice in this matter—he has connected with thousands of couples over the years and has seen it all, as they say. Plus, Bob is so downright practical, you can't wait to apply his insights, especially when it comes to showing love! So, carve out time with this remarkable book, turn the page, and learn to *Love Like You Mean It*. It's *that* life-changing!

Joni Eareckson Tada, Joni and Friends International Disability Center

Our friend, Bob Lepine, knocks it out of the park with his new book, *Love Like You Mean It*. Bob takes readers on an in-depth journey through the "love chapter," 1 Corinthians 13. He unpacks the truth of genuine love given in the words of Scripture and brings to light how each one of us can move forward in becoming more like Christ in our love-life. Written for married and engaged couples, this book also speaks to singles as Bob digs down to explore what characteristics are evidence of true agape love. Thanks, Bob!

Alex and Stephen Kendrick, filmmakers, *War Room* and *Overcomer*

So we *think* we *know* what love is when we first marry . . . then after 12 months or 12,000 miles in our marriage journey we know that what we thought was love, isn't! If you are looking for the real thing, my friend and colleague Bob Lepine, aka "Dr. Love," will be a gentle and fun-loving tutor as he introduces you to love Himself. This is the ultimate how-to book where you can express and experience true love. Buckle up and tighten your seat belt, Dr. Love is going to take you on the ride of your life—and I can promise you this is the *real thing*!

Dr. Dennis Rainey, cofounder of FamilyLife
and TheRaineys.org

Avoiding sentimental clichés, my friend Bob Lepine provides biblical, sensible, practical help in learning what love means.

Alistair Begg, senior pastor,
Parkside Church, Chagrin Falls, Ohio

Grounded in the Scriptures and written by someone who not only has helped tens of thousands of couples but also practices what he preaches, *Love Like You Mean It* is a treasure. This wonderful, timely book reaches past the shallow, superficial definitions and descriptions of love and points us to the foundation of an enduring marriage—an intentional, willful love. Thanks, Bob, for this very helpful book!

Dr. Crawford W. Loritts Jr., author, speaker, radio host, and
senior pastor, Fellowship Bible Church, Roswell, Georgia

Sitting in the radio studio each day with Bob Lepine, we know that we will always get at least two things—solid biblical content and a smile. He is always grounded in the Word and brings joy into every room. This book is no different. Married couples are longing to discover what true love looks like, and Bob delivers from God's Word. As you read you will be smiling because he also brings joy on every page. Enjoy and watch Jesus transform your marriage as you live out these truths.

Dave and Ann Wilson, hosts, *FamilyLife Today*
and authors of *Vertical Marriage*

Love
Like You
Mean
It

BOB
LEPINE

Love Like You Mean It

THE HEART OF A
MARRIAGE
THAT HONORS GOD

Foreword by **Gary Thomas**

PUBLISHING
NASHVILLE, TENNESSEE

Published by B&H Publishing Group
Nashville, Tennessee

Dewey Decimal Classification: 306.81
Subject Heading: LOVE / MARRIAGE / EMOTIONS

Unless otherwise noted, all Scripture is taken from the English
Standard Version (ESV). ESV® Text Edition: 2016. Copyright © 2001
by Crossway Bibles, a publishing ministry of Good News Publishers.

Also used: New International Version (NIV). NIV® Copyright ©1973,
1978, 1984 by Biblica, Inc.® Used by permission. All rights reserved
worldwide.

Also used: The Message (MSG), copyright © 1993, 2002, 2018 by
Eugene H. Peterson

Also used: New Amerian Standard (NASB), Copyright © 1960, 1962, 1963,
1968, 1971, 1972, 1973, 1975, 1977, 1995 by The Lockman Foundation.

Also used: King James Version (KJV); public domain.

Cover typography by Kristi Smith, Juicebox Designs

It is the Publisher's goal to minimize disruption caused by technical
errors or invalid websites. While all links are active at the time of
publication, because of the dynamic nature of the internet, some web
addresses or links contained in this book may have changed and may
no longer be valid. B&H Publishing Group bears no responsibility
for the continuity or content of the external site, nor for that of
subsequent links. Contact the external site for answers to questions
regarding its content.

1 2 3 4 5 6 7 • 24 23 22 21 20

To My Church Family at
Redeemer Community Church in Little Rock
You have modeled for me what it looks like for a local church
body to love one another well.

Acknowledgments

There have been many who have contributed to this book. Most of what you will find helpful in these pages comes from the immeasurable way so many of these people have shaped my own thinking about what the Bible teaches about love and marriage.

In 1992, I sat in a conference room with Dennis Rainey, who asked me one of his trademark questions: "Does marriage and family make you weep and pound the table?"

I told Dennis that theology is what makes me weep and pound the table. To the extent marriage and family is on the heart of God, I said, I am passionate about it.

What I didn't realize in 1992, and what I've come to realize in the years since, is how much marriage and family is on God's heart. Dennis's own passion for these matters has been a key part of helping me see the centrality of marriage and family to God's plan for humanity. During our more than twenty-five years of working together on *FamilyLife Today*, Dennis was both a friend and a mentor. His life marked my life and marked much of what you'll read in this book.

This book has also been shaped through the years by the hundreds of people who I've been fortunate enough to interact with as radio guests on *FamilyLife Today*. Clearly there are too many to name. But having recorded more than six thousand programs, those guests have been the instructors who have helped sharpen my understanding of God's design for marriage.

Along with the radio guests whose fingerprints are on these pages, I am indebted to my friends and collogues at FamilyLife— too many to name—who share a common passion for bringing practical, biblical help and hope to marriages and families all around the world. Special thanks are due to long time teammates Christy Bain, Tonda Nations, Mike Clowers, Emmitt Fowler, Michelle Hill, Mark Ramey, and Keith Lynch.

It's also a great joy and privilege for me to be partnered together with the new hosts of *FamilyLife Today*, my friends Dave and Ann Wilson. Their tireless desire to point people vertical— to Jesus—has challenged and inspired me.

In 2008, God led a small group of men and women, along with my wife and me, to help plant a new church in our city. Our vision was for a church where people would take the Bible seriously, where worship would be heartfelt and passionate, where people would be connected with one another in grace-based, Christ-centered relationships and where individuals and families would live their lives on mission by loving and serving others. I assumed the responsibility as the primary teaching pastor at Redeemer Community Church.

Since the beginning of the church, I've been yoked together in ministry with an amazing group of men who have shared the joys and burdens of local church leadership. This book owes a great debt to these men—Tom Arnold, Tim Friesen, Matt Gurney, Rick Houk, Jim McMurry, Mike Morledge, John Dietrich, and Curtis Thomas. Mark Rens, who graduated to glory in 2011. We all miss him still.

The congregation at Redeemer is an amazing group of people who love Jesus and the gospel. I am a blessed pastor to be called to serve these wonderful people. And I'm grateful to God for preserving the unity of the Spirit in the bonds of peace in our church all these years.

This book has introduced me to new friends—the skilled team at B&H Publishing that has helped give birth to this work. Andy Whisenant, Jenaye White, my editor Taylor Combs, and my literary agent Erik Wolgemuth were key members of that team. I'm also indebted to Robert Wolgemuth who kept asking me over the years, "When are you going to write your next book?" Here it is.

On a practical level, so much of what I've learned about love has come from the people closest to me. My five children—Amy, Katie, James, John, and David have been a source of great joy and pride to me as their father. The Bible says there is no greater joy than to know that our children are walking in the truth (3 John 4). These five children, their spouses, and my nine grandchildren, have demonstrated love for their mom and me and for one another in ways that has made my heart soar. I love you all.

Finally, the words on the pages that follow would be hollow and theoretical if they had not been forged more than forty-plus years of marriage to my wife Mary Ann. On our wedding invitation, we included 1 John 4:19: "We love because he first loved us." Our love for one another has deepened and grown sweeter through the years. More than anyone, she has shaped my understanding of what it means to love sacrificially and generously.

Soli Deo Gloria!

Contents

Foreword

*I*met my wife when we were kids. By the time we married, we had been in the same Sunday school class, we had been on church camping trips together—including a fifty mile canoe trip—and I had mopped the floors at Herfy's Hefty Burgers while she laughed and didn't believe me when I insisted I usually got to cook the burgers. We sat in early morning college classes together, including an excruciatingly boring linguistics class that Lisa, of course, excelled in, and had been through the calendar several times: a day spent playing in the snow at Mt. Baker, autumn walks in the leaves surrounding Sehome Hill Arboretum, spring bonfires on Bellingham Bay, and summer evenings in our respective hometowns. We had gone to watch the state high school cross country championships (which Lisa didn't think was a date but I did). We had been to numerous church services and Campus Christian Fellowship meetings. She had encouraged me when I was shocked and saddened and processing it by volunteering at a Keith Green memorial concert together. Put all of this together, and I had seen Lisa in just about every context you could see someone in. And yet . . .

And yet on our wedding day, she just looked so different.

Watching her walk up the aisle, I wondered, *how could someone so familiar be so excitingly new?* It wasn't just that she was wearing more makeup than usual (she's not much of a makeup person, to be honest; she has a natural beauty all her own). I had never seen her in a wedding dress, never seen her walking up a church aisle to join her hand in mine and, after a few heartfelt promises, kiss me on the lips and say those wonderful words, "I do."

I got a little bit of the same feeling reading Bob Lepine's *Love Like You Mean It*. I've read so many marriage books I've almost become inoculated against their advice. The "Christian marriage book" has practically become a trope. But I was challenged by virtually every paragraph of Bob's marvelous book as if I was reading a Christian marriage book for the very first time.

For instance, rarely has an author grabbed me right off the bat like Bob does here:

> Nobody knows who said it first. But the statement is still true. "Everybody wants to go to heaven. But nobody wants to die." The premise of this book is similar. Everybody wants a marriage that is filled with love. But nobody wants to die to self.

The entire book is wise, seasoned, and mature. You can tell Bob has spoken to many couples and heard from the church's leading and most cherished authors, because he takes the best of them, and then elevates their advice to the next level. That's what I found so amazing about this book.

Another thing that struck me is that because this book is essentially exposition (going through a Bible passage word by word), it carries a power and conviction that so many books simply lack. This isn't a book that comes about from clever marketing gimmicks, or seeks to repackage familiar content with stylish or hip language, or that is based on Bob's opinion of what marriages need today. He draws on a very familiar passage (1 Cor. 13:4ff) but makes it sound and feel astonishingly new—just like Lisa looked to me on our wedding day.

Most marriage books begin and end with what the author thinks is most important: communication, conflict resolution, sexual intimacy, finances, parenting, and so on. *Love Like You Mean It* begins and ends with God's definition of love, and that's what makes it so powerful. In the end, if we pursue love and grow in love (as God defines it) most conflicts, communication struggles, sexual issues, financial concerns, and so on, can be addressed in an entirely new way with an entirely new power from an entirely new platform.

Even if you've read every marriage book published in the last twenty years, you'll still find new inspiration, encouragement, challenge, conviction, and God-breathed hope and wisdom in this fine work. That's why I'm so delighted to recommend it to all believers who want to look at marriage and love—two very familiar words—and rediscover both of them in an entirely new light: God's light.

Gary Thomas
Author of *Sacred Marriage* and *Cherish*

Introduction

*N*obody knows who said it first. But the statement is still true. "Everybody wants to go to heaven. But nobody wants to die."

The premise of this book is similar. Everybody wants a marriage that is filled with love. But nobody wants to die to self.

God created each one of us with a deep longing. We yearn to be fully known and fully loved at the same time. We were created, not to live in isolation, but to be connected to others. Each one of us wants to have people in our lives who "get us," who cheer us on, and who fill in the gaps in our lives. At our core, that's the kind of love we're longing for.

That's the promise that marriage holds out to us.

The first man, Adam, was alone in the garden. After everything God had made up to that point, he proclaimed, "It is good." But when God saw Adam without a partner, God said, "It is not good. I will make a helper for him." And after a divine surgical procedure involving the removal of a rib, God fashioned Adam's suitable helper. Then, in his final act of creation, God took the two and made them one. In doing so, God gave the man and the woman a taste of the same kind of perfect fellowship and love that the three Persons of the Godhead have always experienced and enjoyed. They experienced unhindered, unbroken love.

Most of us expected that a loved-filled marriage would be easy to achieve. Maybe you're not yet married or dating, and you

1

expect that when you find your perfect match, your love for one another will grow automatically deeper and deeper. Or maybe you're recently married or about to be married, and your passions and emotions are easily stirred. At this point in your relationship, love doesn't seem to require any effort on your part. That's why we call it "falling in love." Love just happens naturally, the way we see it happen in Hallmark movies.

The Bible has a word for the kind of love all of us are longing to experience in a marriage. The word is *oneness*. In Genesis 2:24, God tells us that when a man leaves his father and mother and cleaves to his wife, the two become one.

But the kind of perfect "oneness" love that Adam and Eve experienced as a married couple in Genesis 2 didn't last long. Their rebellion against God in Genesis 3 changed everything for them, including their experience of marital love.

And if you've been married for any length of time, you've undoubtedly experienced some of what they experienced.

Most of us at some point are so captivated by the strong emotions associated with romantic love that we miscalculate the impact our sin nature has on our quest for perfect love in marriage. We think marital love will be easy and come quickly. But what we think will be easy turns out to be a lot harder than we expected.

Most of us bring with us into marriage a fairly shallow, superficial view of what love is. We learn about love from rom-coms, Jane Austen and the Brontë sisters, and a sixteenth-century playwright in England who introduced us to a pair of "star-crossed lovers." When you mix movies and novels and poetry and pop songs into a stew pot, what you get is an emotionally charged, exciting mixture that over the years has come to be known as "love."

And that's a problem.

For generations now, men and women have understood that the love shared between a man and a woman is both the foundation for a strong marriage and the source of the deep joy that holds us together in the holy bonds of matrimony. But somewhere along the way, we lost sight of the qualities that define the kind of love that is necessary for a marriage to be what it was designed to be.

As a result, we hear people today saying absurd things like, "I love you, but I'm not in love with you." Which, translated, means "I think you're a decent, nice person. And I have some feelings for you—some kind of concern or care. But I don't feel the spark or the delight I think I'm supposed to feel. I felt it once, a long time ago. But I've lost it."

We have husbands today who wonder why they aren't as attracted to their wives as they are to the cute young woman who shows up at work looking pretty, smiling and laughing at their jokes. And we have wives who wonder what happened to the funny, charming, cute young man who used to spend hours just talking to her and looking deeply in her eyes.

Now, with two kids and two car payments and college debt and full-time jobs and no time just to chill with each other or with friends, husbands and wives who once felt sparks of passion whenever they were together now find themselves feeling empty and lonely and bored, wondering where the love went.

This book is for those who are there. Or for those who think they might one day be there. Or for those who want to avoid ever being there at all costs.

The truth is, in these cases, the love didn't evaporate. It was never really love at all.

We've been sold a bill of goods about what love is. Like products advertised on late-night television that look amazing but never revolutionize our lives the way they promise, we are duped into thinking that when we exchange vows to love one another until death parts us, we're signing up to receive a lifetime supply of passion and affirmation and attention and care.

In fact, if we're really honest, most of us got married because of how our spouse made us feel when we were together. We liked the feeling. So we said, "I'll move in and wear a ring and share a house payment and have kids with you—as long as you keep making me feel that way."

Deep down, we don't get married so that we can love someone else. We get married because we fall in love with the feeling of being loved. Most of us get married to get, not to give.

Meanwhile, we have right in front of us the whole time the portrait of the kind of rugged, committed love that may not sell a lot of movie tickets or romance novels, but that sustains marriages in good times and bad. Some of us even had the description of this kind of rugged love read at our weddings. With friends and family assembled, someone opened a Bible to 1 Corinthians 13 and started to read what sounded at the time like love poetry. They read about the tongues of angels and noisy gongs. They read about bearing all things, believing all things, hoping all things, and enduring all things. In the midst of our big day, it all sounded wonderful and magical.

But if we had been listening carefully to what they were reading, we would have heard a description of a kind of love and loyalty that, as songwriter Rich Mullins said, goes deeper than mere sentiment. A kind of steadfast, enduring love that is the most commonly mentioned attribute of God in all of Scripture. A kind of self-sacrificing, self-denying love that Jesus defined as the "greater love" (John 15:13) and that he demonstrated for us by dying in our place (Rom. 5:8).

I like romance and passion as much as the next person. They are the seasoning that makes a marriage relationship vibrant. There is a reason people talk about "spicing up" a marriage. Romance and passion add a zest and joy that bring delight and desire to marriage.

But the foundation for a marriage that endures is not passion and desire. It's love. Real love. The kind of love that the apostle Paul described for everyone who was part of the church that gathered in the ancient city of Corinth. These were passionate, impulsive new believers whose pagan background was mixed together with a newfound zeal for God. The outcome of that zeal without knowledge was problematic.

So Paul wrote to this young church to teach them about a kind of love they didn't understand. A kind of love that was just as unknown in their day as it is in ours.

While the Bible's description of love in 1 Corinthians 13 did not have the husband/wife relationship as its focus, this portrait of genuine love perfectly describes and defines the kind of love that God has in mind for every married couple.

This book is my attempt to get us back on track when it comes to understanding what real love is and how we live it out in marriage. If you're looking for quick fixes and superficial adjustments you can make that will cause love to flourish in your marriage, send this book back and ask for a refund. What we see in Scripture is that the kind of deep love for which our souls long does not come through tweaking. It's a long, slow, rigorous process.

But what the Bible promises us is this: the kind of greater love found here is the pathway to joy. It's the real thing. It's the kind of love that will bring real, deep-down, soul-level contentment. The imitation love that the world is peddling will never get you there. It will spring up and fade quickly. Real love takes time. It takes work. There are no shortcuts. But in the end, it's the only love that satisfies.

My hope is that this study of Paul's definition of love in 1 Corinthians 13 can help us learn to love our spouse in a way that goes farther and deeper than momentary sparks of passion or romance.

And my hope is that as you take time to ponder and consider the characteristics of the bold, rugged, genuine love described in 1 Corinthians 13, you'll think on these things with a soft, humble, teachable heart. And that as you read this book, you'll read it with the prayer from Psalm 139:

> Search me, O God, and know my heart!
> Try me and know my thoughts!
> And see if there be any grievous way in me,
> and lead me in the way everlasting!
> (vv. 23–24)

My hope is also that the elements of genuine love found in 1 Corinthians 13 would increasingly become the elements of genuine love that you aspire to as you get married or that you manifest in your marriage now. I hope you're ready to go on a journey that's designed to help you become a more loving spouse—a journey that will, in the process, strengthen and deepen your love for your mate and revolutionize your marriage.

It's time to understand what real love looks like.

CHAPTER 1

Everything Minus Love = Nothing

*Y*ou can have a nice marriage without the kind of "greater love" that the Bible describes. But there will always be something missing. And it won't be a marriage that glorifies God.

> If I speak in the tongues of men and of angels,
> but have not love,
> I am a noisy gong
> or a clanging cymbal.
> And if I have prophetic powers,
> and understand all mysteries and all
> knowledge,
> and if I have all faith,
> so as to remove mountains,
> but have not love,
> I am nothing.
> If I give away all I have,
> and if I deliver up my body to be burned,
> but have not love,
> I gain nothing. (1 Cor. 13:1–3)

It didn't take long for me to be smitten.

I met my wife, Mary Ann, when we were both college students at the University of Tulsa. We were at a weekend retreat together with three or four dozen other students, and we were in line for dinner. Something sparked a conversation between the two of us in that food line, and I noticed that some kind of endorphin rush was happening.

Sounds cheesy, I know. But that's what happened. I liked her smile. I liked her spunk. And I remember liking the way she looked in the red T-shirt she was wearing. I said to myself that night, *I think I'd like to get to know her better.*

Within two months we were dating, and I was carelessly tossing around the "L" word without any regard for what it really meant. To me, saying, "I love you," to someone was essentially the same as saying, "I enjoy your company and I like the way I feel when I'm with you and I hope you'll stop dating other people and agree to date me exclusively so I can keep feeling this way until I get tired of you." I was clearly attaching a shallow meaning to a deep word. But I wasn't alone. I obviously had a lot to learn about what real love is. Thankfully, the Bible gives clarity in, among other places, the opening verses of 1 Corinthians 13.

What's surprising to me is how many husbands and wives have stood before God and witnessed and pledged their undying love to one another without thinking carefully about all that they are signing up for. And it's equally surprising how many people talk about "falling out of love" or no longer being "in love" without considering how the Bible defines what they say they're falling out of.

I think it's time for husbands and wives to read the fine print. Carefully. It's time to look at exactly what you're signing up for when you promise to love someone exclusively for the rest of your life.

It's time to re-up, to dig deeper into the Bible, to begin to understand and apply what the Bible says about love.

Talk Together

1. If you are married or in a relationship, what is one way your understanding of love has changed since the relationship began?

2. Read 1 Corinthians 13:4–7. Tell your spouse which of the qualities of real love listed in the passage is a quality he or she is living out in your marriage.

I know it sounds odd, but I think I actually remember the first time I read 1 Corinthians 13.

It was not in church. It was not during a quiet time. It was not at a wedding.

It was in a head shop.

Some of you have no idea what a head shop is. That's because you are not a child of the sixties. I am. In fact, in the fall of 1968, when Otis Redding was sitting on the dock of the bay and Grace

Slick was telling us all to feed our heads, I had just matriculated to Nipher Junior High School in Kirkwood, Missouri, after a storied career at Henry Hough Elementary School.

Nipher was about two and a half miles from where I lived. Each morning, we carpooled to school, with different moms doing the driving. But when school was out at 3:25 each afternoon, we walked home. Can you believe that? I had to walk two and a half miles from school to my house every day! Carrying my books! Under my arms! (We didn't have fancy backpacks when I was a boy!)

The good news is that the path home took me right by the Dairy Queen. I would regularly stop for a $.45 cent Old Fashioned Chocolate Ice Cream soda to sustain me on my long journey.

How old do I sound right now?

Sometime during my junior high years, a new store opened just past the Diary Queen on Kirkwood Road. I don't remember the name of the store. It may not have had a name. Didn't matter.

It was a head shop.

If that's a new category for you, here is how Wikipedia defines a *head shop*:

> A head shop is a retail outlet specializing in paraphernalia used for consumption of canna-
> bis and tobacco items related to cannabis cul-
> ture and related countercultures. Products may
> include magazines (e.g., about cannabis cul-
> ture, cannabis cultivation, tattooing and music),
> clothing, and home décor (e.g., posters and wall
> hangings illustrating drug culture themes such
> as cannabis, jam bands like The Grateful Dead,
> psychedelic art, etc.).[1]

I was a clean-cut suburban boy who didn't know much about cannabis culture or psychedelics beyond what I had seen on TV or heard about on the new FM rock music radio station that everyone had started listening to. So I was not part of the target market for the new head shop. But I was curious.

So one day, after polishing off my chocolate ice cream soda from Dairy Queen, I worked up the courage to go inside. I remember that in the middle of the afternoon, the store was dark, like they didn't want you to see what was for sale. There was some funky jewelry. A lot of fringed leather jackets. Incense. Rolling papers and other smoking paraphernalia. Lots of black lights and florescent posters. Hendrix. Joplin. Peter Max.

And that's where I first read 1 Corinthians 13.

The first eight verses of the chapter were hanging on a poster on the wall that was right next to another poster that proclaimed, "You are a child of the universe, no less than the trees and stars, you have a right to be here."

An odd setting for displaying one of the best-known chapters in the Bible, right?

The reason there was a poster for 1 Corinthians 13 in a head shop in 1968 is because there was widespread confusion then, as now, about love. The year 1967 had already happened and had become known as the Summer of Love. The Beatles had told us that "All We Need Is Love." And we were just months away from the Woodstock Music and Art Fair on Max Yasgur's farm in upstate New York that promised us peace, love, and music.

But the love that was being promoted in the sixties was not the same love that the apostle Paul had in mind when he wrote his letter to an ancient church that was infected with the pagan spirit of their age. When Paul wrote 1 Corinthians 13, he wrote to a church in a culture where the definition of love had more in common with Woodstock than with Jesus.

Kind of like where our culture is today.

Talk Together

1. How do you think most people in our culture define love today?

2. Do you think Paul wrote to the Corinthian church about the characteristics of real love primarily to inspire them? To inform them? To correct them? Explain your answer.

Paul wrote this letter to this church in this culture for a reason. In chapter 13 in particular, he was communicating two overarching themes. First, he was making it clear for his readers that love is at the center of what it means to be a follower of Jesus. A loveless Christian is an oxymoron. It's a contradiction in terms.

And second, Paul wanted to drive home the message that God's definition of love is radically different than what most of us think of when we think about love. Paul wrote 1 Corinthians 13 to contrast the way the people in the church in Corinth were associating with one another with what he describes as the "more excellent way" (1 Cor. 12:31). The Corinthians related to one another through their gifts, abilities, and strengths. They valued others based on how gifted the other person was. Some gifts earned you more honor than others.

Paul spent 1 Corinthians 12 talking about the value and importance of spiritual gifts. He explained that Christians need to love one another and that we all benefit when we are using the gifts God has given us not for our own glory, but to encourage and serve one another.

But he also pointed out how having a wrong perspective on spiritual gifts can destroy relationships. Gifts without love, he said, are nothing but a lot of unpleasant noise.

The "more excellent way" Paul advanced in 1 Corinthians 13 is a way of living that puts self-sacrificing, self-denying concern for and care of others at the center of relationships. Jesus said that at the core of everything in the Bible, there are two commands: loving God and loving others. Those two priorities are the "more excellent way" that should drive every aspect of our lives.

To capture the attention of his readers, Paul used a unique word: *agape.*

If you've been a Christian for any length of time, that Greek word—*agape*—is a word you've no doubt heard. Theologian J. I. Packer says the word "seems to have been virtually a Christian invention—a new word for a new thing."[2] In fact, apart from about twenty occurrences in the Greek version of the Old Testament, the word *agape* is almost nonexistent in Greek culture before the New Testament.

Packer says, "Agape draws its meaning directly from the revelation of God in Christ. It is not a form of natural affection, however intense, but a supernatural fruit of the Spirit (Gal. 5:22). It is a matter of will rather than feeling (for Christians must love even those they dislike—Matt. 5:44–48) . . . It is the basic element in Christ-likeness."[3]

John Stott defines *agape* love this way: it is the sacrifice of self in the service of another.[4] This kind of love, he says, is a servant of the will, not a victim of the emotions.

And Alistair Begg says that what we're talking about when we talk about *agape* love is not "coziness, affection [or] predisposition on the basis of attraction." *Agape*, he says, is a spiritual discipline.[5]

Think for just a minute about how these ways of thinking about love will recalibrate the way we interact with one another in marriage. The vow to "love, honor, and cherish" your spouse is not a vow to *feel* a certain way about your spouse for a lifetime. Instead, it's a vow to choose to act in a certain way toward your spouse for a lifetime. It's a vow that you promise to keep "for better, for worse, for richer, for poorer, in sickness and in health for as long as you both shall live."

Back in the sixties the "free love" movement wasn't about *agape*. It was about *eros*—a different Greek word that refers to romantic or sexual love. The same was true in Corinth. The Greeks saw sexual love as the highest expression of love for another person.

And that way of thinking about love is still part of our culture twenty centuries later. We think about love today in terms of passion, romance, and sex, not in terms of self-sacrifice or placing someone else's needs ahead of our own.

The apostle Paul was not the first to use this new idea of *agape* to correct misguided cultural ideas about love in his day. Jesus gave his disciples a helpful way of getting to the core of what *agape* looks like: "Greater love has no one than this, that someone lay down his life for his friends" (John 15:13).

And John the apostle reminds his readers that Jesus didn't just talk about what *agape* looks; he lived it. "This is how we know what love is: Jesus Christ laid down his life for us" (1 John 3:16 NIV).

Agape love is one of the defining characteristics of Christianity. Sacrificing yourself to serve others is not at the center of any other world religion as it is with Christianity. And that was certainly true in Paul's day. The Greeks, the Romans, and the ancient Middle Eastern pagan religions made no claim that their gods were loving or that they commanded people to serve them by loving others.

In our day, where *eros* love has become the common understanding of what love means, an *agape*-centered Christian marriage gives us an opportunity to show a watching world that we serve a God who defines love differently, who demonstrated for us what self-sacrificing love is all about, and who empowers us to supernaturally, sacrificially love one another.

Talk Together

1. If it's true that "a loveless Christian is an oxymoron," is it also true that a loveless Christian marriage is a contradiction? Explain why or why not?

2. Talk about John Stott's statement that love is "a servant of the will, not a victim of the emotions." Is that true for you?

This "more excellent way" of love that the apostle Paul describes for us in 1 Corinthians 13 is revolutionary, not just for marriage, but for all of life. It's at the center of how we are to function as God's children.

That's what these verses tell us. God, in Christ, pours his love into us. He loves us with an everlasting, steadfast, and enduring love. And as the recipients of his love, we are to be a conduit of his love to each other.

In other words, God loves us not simply for our own benefit, but so that as we are filled up with his love for us, we can pour out his love to one another.

Paul begins his description of this "more excellent way" of love in 1 Corinthians 13 by listing a number of abilities or activities that we would commonly associate with spiritually mature people. The picture he paints for us in the first three verses of 1 Corinthians 13 is a picture of people who would be recognized in any era as being spiritual standouts. A cut above everyone else. He peppers his prose with exaggeration and hyperbole to drive home his point.

And then he delivers the knockout blow.

A person who loves others with self-sacrificing *agape* love, Paul writes, is more faithfully following Jesus than someone who is exercising his or her spiritual gifts absent of *agape* love.

Here's the formula Paul is proposing:

Extraordinary giftedness – *Agape* love = Nothing.

Let that sink in for a minute.

Paul says you can do everything right in life, in marriage, in seeking to serve God, and if there is no *agape* love at the center of it all, you have nothing. You don't have something "less than." You have nothing. You have exactly zero.

What that means for marriage is clear. You can be a responsible, charming, attractive, fun-loving successful, intelligent, respected individual, admired and esteemed by everyone. You can be, by all standards, an ideal spouse. But if your marriage is not fueled by a strong and durable commitment to sacrificially love your mate, it's not a Christian marriage. It's a façade.

Phil Ryken says we need to keep in mind that "no one will hear the gospel from the life of a loveless Christian. People just hear 'bong, bong, bong, clang, clang, clang.'"[6] And no one will see the gospel in the life of a loveless marriage.

Are you gifted and using your gifts in your marriage, but without love? Paul says what you're doing amounts to nothing.

Do you have knowledge and understanding of Scripture, but lack love? Paul says your knowledge is worth nothing.

Do you have great faith, trusting and obeying God, but no love? Your faith is worthless. It's nothing.

You starting to see a pattern here?

But Paul doesn't stop there. He goes so far as to say that not every act of self-sacrifice or self-denial is a demonstration of *agape* love.

Do you think it's possible for someone to give away all he or she has out of self-interest? Is it possible that the motivation for self-denial can actually be self-serving? Or to put a finer point on it, is it possible to have a self-centered motivation for putting the interests of your spouse ahead of your own interests?

In 1997, TV mogul Ted Turner announced that he was giving a gift of $1 billion to the United Nations to support humanitarian concerns. His gift was detailed in an article entitled "Ted Turner: The First Man of Philanthropy." Here is in part what it said:

> He has a philanthropic soul and has always been an incredibly generous benefactor. His most astounding single grant was $1 billion to form the United Nations Foundation which works in concert with the United Nations, to serve global humanitarian needs through verbal, non-violent resolutions.[7]

The article that praises Turner as a man with a philanthropic soul can be found online at Ted Turner.com.

I don't know Ted Turner's heart. And I am not his judge. But as this online article indicates, it's possible to give away a lot of money with at least some of the motivation being that everyone knows what a generous guy you are. At the very least, there is a smidgen of self-interest mixed in with Ted Turner's philanthropy.

Some people give away lots of money to ease their conscience. Others give away lots of money because they think a life of poverty will please God. The apostle Paul says if you give away all you have and you are motivated by something other than love, here is what you have earned for yourself from God: Nothing.

The most radical extent to which Paul takes this argument is that even those who are willingly martyred for their faith may have wrong motives. Martyrdom was a present reality for the Christians to whom Paul was writing this letter. And the apostle wanted to make sure that none of his readers would embrace the false idea that martyrdom for your faith is a sure ticket to heaven.

So, here's the picture Paul paints. If you are someone who is gifted, eloquent, bold, full of faith, full of understanding and insight, generous, and committed to the extent that you are ready to give your life for your faith, we might assume you are a solid, committed follower of Jesus. But without love, everything else is N.O.T.H.I.N.G.

What is it that defines, more than anything, the person and ministry of Jesus? After all, he did all the things Paul is talking about in 1 Corinthians. What were the miracles? The faith? The martyrdom?

Read back through that last paragraph. Some words are missing . . .

You know the answer. It's the love. His love for us. He went to the cross not as a martyr but as a savior. He went to lay down his life for his friends. He went to rescue us. He went because of his great love for all who would die to self and follow him.

And in order for you to be a dispenser of the kind of love described in 1 Corinthians 13, you have to first be a receiver of God's love for you. You have to recognize that you have lived a life in rebellion against God. A life focused first and foremost on yourself. Your life has been committed to you.

And the Bible says that while you and I were still in a state of being committed to our own self-interests, God demonstrated his great love for us in this—Christ died for us.

What does the hymn say? Jesus emptied himself of all but what? *Love.* He bled for Adam's helpless race. "Amazing love, how can it be, that thou, my God shouldst die for me."[8]

The character qualities that define *agape* love listed in 1 Corinthians 13 are not some kind of self-improvement checklist. They are descriptors of the kind of love that God has for us, and that is produced by the Holy Spirit in the hearts of those whose lives are being transformed.

The more we realize the depth of God's love for us, and the more we meditate on how we are recipients of God's grace and love for us, the more we will begin to grow in grace and love for others.

Your marriage will only be built on a foundation of *agape* love if both of you are growing in your understanding of God's love and grace for you.

The kind of love the Bible describes in 1 Corinthians 13 is not essential for a couple to have a happy marriage. That statement may shock you, but it's true. There are plenty of couples who have negotiated a workable arrangement in marriage that is mutually satisfying. Adjustments are made, basic desires are met, and everyone is comfortable with the setup.

But God's goal for us in marriage goes far beyond comfort and mutual satisfaction. God's goal for marriage is that we would taste something deeper, something sweeter, and something more glorious in our marriages. He wants us to experience the kind of joy that the Father, Son, and Spirit have always known from long before the world began. He wants us to experience the profound joy that comes from a kind of oneness that is only found in him. And the only path that leads to that kind of soul-satisfying oneness and joy is the path where the kind of love described here is being cultivated and is flourishing.

When that happens in marriage, we'll know a kind of joy and contentment we've never known before. And God will be exalted in the process because we'll be showing to everyone around us that his ways are perfect and right and true.

Talk Together

1. Have you ever known someone who showed some evidence of spiritual maturity but who lacked love? And have you ever known someone who lacked elements of spiritual maturity but whose life demonstrated sacrificial love for others? Compare those two lives.

2. When did you begin to understand the reality of God's love for you? What role did your understanding of your own sin play?

CHAPTER 2

An Odd Place to Begin:
Love Is Patient

Love is patient.
(1 Cor. 13:4a)

*T*he first test of how we love each other in marriage is how we relate to one another in the middle of trials and adversity.

Maria and Hector[1] sat across from me at the dinner table. It was our first night of premarital counseling, and they were nervous and excited about their upcoming wedding and their new life together.

I handed both of them a blank sheet of paper and asked them to take five minutes to write a paragraph for me. I wanted to know how they would define the word *love*.

What I got back from them that night sounded like a cross between a Hallmark greeting card and some bad poetry written in the 1960s. It was all mush and sentiment. It was all about the incomprehensible, unfathomable, and mysterious ways that being in love makes us feel.

Don't get me wrong. I'm as much of a sucker for mush and sentiment as the next person. But as I read what these two had written, I realized that since this couple was about to pledge their undying devotion to one another, I needed to help them come up with a more durable definition of love than the definition they had in their heads.

In 1967, Kim Grove was a twenty-six-year-old woman from New Zealand, now living in Los Angeles, working as a receptionist for a design firm. That year, she met and fell in love with an Italian-born computer engineer named Roberto Casali at a ski club where they were both taking lessons.

When Roberto started working in San Francisco, Kim began to write him daily love letters. At the end of each of those letters, she drew a cartoon of the two of them hand in hand or cuddling or kissing. Under the pictures, she wrote, "Love is . . ." and then she completed the sentence with a sentimental description. "Love is when it's great being together." "Love is when little things mean a lot." "Love is sharing the housework." And so on.

Someone at Kim's office saw one of her cartoons and liked it. That led Kim to start making booklets of her drawings which she sold for $1. Eventually, someone from the *Los Angeles Times* got ahold of one of the booklets, and in January of 1970, the newspaper published the first of Kim Grove's "Love Is" cartoons.

Before long, Kim's doodling and romantic ideals became a worldwide phenomenon, with "Love Is" glasses and mugs and notepads and buttons creating a short-lived but lucrative empire.

Mary Ann and I had a "Love Is" glass in our cupboard for many years.

Neither she nor I can remember the inscription.

The way Kim Grove defined love in her daily comics is very different than the way the apostle Paul defined love in 1 Corinthians 13. There, we find more than a dozen descriptive words or phrases that drain the sentiment from love, dressing it instead in work boots and a hard hat. *These verses are meant not simply to describe what love is, but more accurately, to explain how love acts or what love does.*

The apostle Paul begins his description of love with an unusual attribute. Love, he writes, is patient.

We have a somewhat truncated view of patience. We think of not responding with anger or frustration when something takes longer than expected. We think of instructing our children to sit quietly when they start to fidget or squirm because they're bored. But in the ancient world, patience was something much bigger.

The word translated *patient* in the New Testament is a Greek word that literally means "to put one's anger or wrath far away." The older translations use the term *long-suffering* here, and that how Strong's Dictionary of New Testament Words defines *patient* too. To be patient is "to suffer long, be long-suffering, as opposed to hasty anger or punishment, to forbear, to endure patiently as opposed to losing faith or giving up."[2] Theologian Charles Hodge said that patience "bears with provocation, and is not quick to assert its rights or resent an injury."[3]

What an odd place to begin a description of love. It's almost as if Paul is saying, "Let's get to the bad news first." To demonstrate love, you're going to have to hang tough when things get really hard. You're going to have to put anger out of reach. Love will require that you respond to adversity "with all humility and gentleness, with patience, bearing with one another in love, eager to maintain the unity of the Spirit in the bond of peace" (Eph. 4:2–3).

That's not just an unusual way to respond. It's supernatural.

Talk Together

1. What novel, TV show, or movie would you say has most influenced your understanding of what love in marriage should look like?

2. What one word would you insert here: "A loving person is a _____ person?" Is the word that first came to mind one of the words found in 1 Corinthians 13:4–7?

It doesn't take long for us to try one another's patience in marriage. By the time most of us say, "I do," each of us has at least a couple decades of accumulated idiosyncrasies that we bring with us to the altar. We have expectations of one another. We have patterns of how we think life ought to be.

Early in marriage, those different ways of thinking can easily clash. Expectations we didn't even know we had begin to emerge. We may never have realized how firmly or passionately we feel about the right way to position a roll of toilet paper or to squeeze a tube of toothpaste until we find ourselves sharing a bathroom

AN ODD PLACE TO BEGIN: LOVE IS PATIENT

with someone who either doesn't care enough to do these things correctly, or worse yet, thinks that their *wrong* way of doing them is somehow the right way!

We may be tempted to dismiss these kinds of things as minor annoyances. But learning to cultivate patience as we respond to small things will prepare us for the bigger challenges. Even trivial issues can be like termites in a marriage. Small and hidden, these seemingly minor aggravations can eat away at love in a relationship. Over the years, I've met couples whose marriages have ended because of an accumulation of seemingly minor irritations that ultimately left them isolated and angry with each other.

The idea that real love involves grace and perseverance in the face of genuine suffering raises all kinds of questions for married couples. Is the Bible calling us to suffer silently when our spouse is the source of that suffering? When we vowed to have and to hold for better or worse, how much "worse" does God expect a husband or wife to faithfully endure? Are we stretching the meaning of patience too far when we start talking about actual suffering and not just being gracious about things like toothpaste tubes and toilet paper rolls?

The posture of patience is a proactive, grace-giving posture. It's a posture that defaults to grace. In writing to people who were experiencing suffering because of their faith, the apostle Peter pressed his readers to bear up under the weight of the persecution. It "is a gracious thing," Peter said, "when, mindful of God, one endures sorrows while suffering unjustly" (1 Pet. 2:19). Don't give into the impulses of the flesh (1 Pet. 2:11). Don't repay evil for evil, but give a blessing instead. Watch what you say—don't sin with your tongue. Seek peace. If you suffer for righteousness' sake, you will be blessed (1 Pet. 3:9–14). Be self-controlled. Be sober-minded. And keep on "loving one another earnestly, since love covers a multitude of sins" (1 Pet. 4:7–8).

Peter's charge in these verses mirrors what he heard Jesus say. Turn the other cheek. Go the second mile. Love your enemies. Pray for them (Matt. 5:38–48).

What would your marriage look like if you made it your aim, in the power of the Holy Spirit, to live out this kind of radical patience for your spouse? Read back through the last two paragraphs with your marriage in mind, and ask yourself the question: "Do these things describe me?"

This is what patience looks like. It's what love looks like. It should be our default posture as followers of Jesus.

Consider the patience of God toward us. The psalmist declares that God is "slow to anger and abounding in steadfast love" (Ps. 103:8). When God spoke to Moses on Mt. Sinai, he declared that he was "a God merciful and gracious, slow to anger, and abounding in steadfast love and faithfulness" (Exod. 34:6).

God is patient when we sin against him. Someone has said that sin would have fewer takers if its consequences were immediate! But the Bible says God is patient in judgment, giving us every opportunity for repentance (2 Pet. 3:9).

Jesus' life was a picture of patience. He was never married, so we can't look at how he related to a wife to see a model of what marital love should look like (although the Bible does use the metaphor of marriage to describe Jesus' relationship with his bride, the church). But the characteristics of love found in 1 Corinthians 13 were clearly on display as Jesus interacted with his disciples.

Jesus modeled patience in the way he corrected Peter each time he put his foot in his mouth. When James and John were arguing about who would get to sit where in the kingdom, Jesus did not become angry or respond with sarcasm. He responded with patience as he taught then about humility.

And think about this for a minute. Jesus was even patient toward Judas.

In fact, as you think about ways your spouse may have wronged you in your marriage, consider what we can learn from Jesus and Judas. Judas was the betrayer. He was fully complicit in the death of Jesus. Jesus knew what was in Judas's heart as they sat together eating the Passover meal. When Jesus announced to his disciples that one of them would betray him, he knew exactly which one it would be.

Later that same night, after Judas had left the others, the disciples were gathered for prayer in a garden just outside the walls of the city of Jerusalem. Matthew says, "Judas came, one of the twelve, and with him a great crowd with swords and clubs, from the chief priests and the elders of the people" (Matt. 26:47).

That's not what the disciples had been praying would happen. It's not what you hope happens at your prayer meeting.

Matthew says that Judas identified Jesus for the authorities by walking right up to him and using a predetermined sign. "He came up to Jesus at once and said, 'Greetings, Rabbi!' And he kissed him" (v. 49). He used a sign of affection and endearment to signal to local law enforcement that this was the man they wanted for execution.

Jesus, who knew what was in Judas's heart and could see right through his hypocrisy, did not erupt with anger. He didn't respond with sarcasm. He didn't give a stinging rebuke.

Instead, "Jesus said to him, 'Friend, do what you came to do'" (v. 50).

Friend?

That's the remarkable, long-suffering love of Jesus on display.

Jesus' followers were not as patient. When the temple guards came to seize Jesus, Peter—the same apostle who went on to write a letter about how to endure suffering—was ready to fight back. He drew a sword and sliced off one of the guard's ears.

In that moment, Jesus again demonstrated great patience. He told Peter to put his sword away. "Do you think that I cannot appeal to my Father, and he will at once send me more than twelve legions of angels? But how then should the Scriptures be fulfilled, that it must be so?" (vv. 53–54). Jesus, who possessed both the power and the authority to defend himself from these attackers, was instead ready to patiently endure what was happening in order to do the will of his Father.

Of course, the arrest in the garden was not the end of Jesus' persecution. After false witnesses perjured themselves and a guilty verdict against Jesus had been announced, the temple guards turned cruel and vicious. "They spit in his face and struck him. And some slapped him, saying, 'Prophesy to us, you Christ! Who is it that struck you?'" (vv. 67–68).

If that were you, and it were in your power to put an end to it, what would you have done? Jesus was patient. He knew God was in control. He knew God was at work. He was there on a mission, and suffering was part of that mission. So he endured. He suffered long.

Talk Together

1. How does thinking about God's patience toward you affect how you demonstrate patience toward your spouse?

2. How do patience and accountability work together side by side? What does impatient accountability look like? What does patience without accountability look like?

We will sin against each other in marriage. It's inevitable. And our sin will bring suffering and pain into our relationship. We will experience disappointment, loneliness, and sorrow as a result of something our spouse has done, sometimes inadvertently and sometimes intentionally. As we follow Jesus and seek to love our spouse by being patient, there will be times when that will mean we must bear the weight of having been sinned against.

And most of the time, patience will mean that we choose to overlook the kinds of common slights we experience in marriage. Proverbs 19:11 is a great marriage verse: "Good sense makes one slow to anger, and it is his glory to overlook an offense." This is what it means to show each other grace in marriage. In the midst of the minor slights or offenses that can occur daily, we don't allow those actions or words to get lodged in our hearts. We absorb the offense, give our spouse grace, and move on.

But there are times when patiently enduring an offense is not the most loving thing we can do. We have to be careful that our willingness to endure doesn't wind up enabling another person to persist in a destructive pattern of sin in their own life. We are not loving another person well if we make it easy for them to continue sinning.

Jan Welch faced this dilemma in her marriage.[4]

Jan first noticed Ron when they were both students in college. He was bright and personable and she was quickly attracted to him. When Ron said it might be nice if the two of them went out for dinner, Jan was quick to respond. On that very first date, Ron said, "I think we need to go look at wedding rings!" Five days later, Ron and Jan were engaged!

Caught up in the euphoria of their engagement, Jan found herself overlooking Ron's jealousy. He became agitated if Jan spent time with friends she had known before she met him. He wanted everything in her life to now revolve around the two of them. And Jan went along.

It wasn't long after they married before Ron made it clear to his wife that he wanted her to stay home while he was at work. He was fine with her leaving their apartment to deliver dinner to him at work. But Ron was insistent that she not go anywhere else during the day without his knowledge and approval. If she did, he would become angry, telling her it wasn't safe for her to be out on her own.

Jan learned to acquiesce, because if she didn't comply, Ron would become enraged. She learned that if she rocked the boat, the outcome was worse than if she just went along with his wishes and worked to keep the peace. So for more than a decade,

Jan Welch lived with an angry, insecure, controlling husband who micromanaged every detail of her day. Why? "I had made a commitment," Jan said. "I grew up as a divorced kid, and I did not want that. I would have rather been unhappy—which I was—than to be happy and not with him . . . I just tried to get through it the best way that I could, because I really loved him. I saw so much good in him, but what I felt was just very empty." Ultimately, Jan said, she simply made peace with her situation. "This is the road I chose. This is the man I chose."[5]

Is Jan's story a picture of patience in a difficult marriage? Or should Jan have done more to stand up for herself in response to her husband's controlling behavior?

I think the answer to both questions is "yes." Yes, Jan persevered and endured in her marriage, without giving up. For whatever reason, she remained patient in the midst of her own suffering.

And in the times when Jan did try to lovingly confront her husband's behavior, the confrontation always ended in anger and blame shifting.

The Bible does not teach that a spouse who is being abused is to remain patient and passive. If the abuse is physical, a spouse's first objective has to be to seek protection. Pick up the phone. Call 911. Let the police do what God intends for police to do—to protect and serve (Rom. 13:1–4).

It's easy from a distance to second-guess how Jan should have responded to her husband in her particular circumstance. But the dilemma she faced points to an important biblical principle: there are times when the most loving thing we can do for

LOVE LIKE YOU MEAN IT

someone else is to humbly confront the pattern of sin we see in their life.

James 5 makes that clear: "My brothers, if anyone among you wanders from the truth and someone brings him back, let him know that whoever brings back a sinner from his wandering will save his soul from death and will cover a multitude of sins" (vv. 19–20).

There will be times when the most loving thing we can do when our spouse is habitually sinning against us is not to enable that sin, but to follow the counsel found in Galatians 6:1: "If anyone is caught in any transgression, you who are spiritual should restore him in a spirit of gentleness. Keep watch on yourself, lest you too be tempted."

Patience is not the same as passivity. Jesus was not passive with the money-changers in the temple. He was patient with the Pharisees, but that didn't keep him from ultimately pronouncing judgment on them (Matt. 23).

Being long-suffering does not mean always overlooking a sin or remaining silent. When God's glory was under attack, Jesus did not hold his tongue. When the gospel was being distorted, he spoke up. His words were bold and direct, but never rooted in pride and never self-serving. He did not sin with his tongue.

So how can we know whether we should overlook a sin or confront it? Here are a few thoughts:

- Before you decide to confront your spouse, make sure you've spent time in prayer, asking God to do a work. It's the Holy Spirit's job to convict us of sin. Ask him to do the work without you needing to say anything.

- Before you decide to confront your spouse, seek wise counsel from godly friends, being careful as you do that you are not gossiping or slandering your spouse.
- Ask yourself what your motive for confrontation is. Is it to help your spouse be able to deal with a sin pattern? Or is there something more self-serving at work?
- If you decide confrontation is required, make sure you spend more time in prayer, this time asking the Holy Spirit to help you speak the truth in love to your spouse.
- Read Colossians 3:8–9 and Ephesians 4:1–3 before you say anything to your spouse.
- Ask yourself what you will do if your spouse becomes angry or defensive. Be prepared for that possibility and be ready to call a temporary time-out before you move forward.
- Be open to correction you may need to hear about your own sin patterns in the process. Be clothed in humility.

Confronting sin in another person is never easy and usually uncomfortable. But if our goal is love, confrontation will occasionally be necessary.

In Jan's case, anytime she attempted to confront her husband's controlling behavior, the confrontation ended poorly.

So she persevered with patience, praying and hoping for a breakthrough.

And eventually, the breakthrough came. Here's how Ron remembers God getting his attention:

> I started seeing my sons treat [my wife] the way I treated her. They would tell her: "Go get this," or "Pick me up now," or "Do this." I'd give them the lecture of: "Well, hey, you're not supposed to talk to your mother that way. This isn't the right . . ." I recall, as vividly as if it was yesterday, God just slapped me across the face and said, "Who do you think they are learning it from?!" because I was teaching them not to value women, not to value their mother—to order people around. That was the moment, I think, when I started realizing, "Something has to change," because there was such inconsistency in what I said I believed and how I was acting.
>
> I started thinking about the people who talked about how much I like to be in control or I always had to be right. I started realizing that I had been mainly a kind of a cognitive Christian most of my life—I had said all the right things, done all the right things—I followed all the appropriate descriptions of what Christian men were supposed to be. But the relationship in my heart with Christ that would transform me, from the inside out, was really

not there. I wasn't submitting myself to anyone, including God.

Ron and Jan's marriage today is an example of the power of patience and prayer to bring about real change. Ron serves today on the faculty at Denver Seminary. In 2014, he wrote a book called *The Controlling Husband* (Baker/Revell) in which he shares his own story and provides help for couples with control issues. Ron is a licensed clinical psychologist, and he and Jan work with couples through Transformational Marriage Counseling and Seminars (transformational-marriage.com). Today, the Welches are doing what 2 Corinthians 1 teaches all of us to do: comforting others in their afflictions with the same comfort they themselves have received from God (v. 4).

This is possible all because Jan chose to be a long-suffering wife, to cling to God, and to be patient.

Talk Together

1. If you are married, what is one way your spouse thinks or acts that came as a surprise once you were married? How did you respond?

2. If you are not yet married, spend some time examining your own habits and routines. What are some things that you may never think twice about that may not seem so normal to a potential spouse?

According to my mom, when I was a little boy and she told me she was taking me shopping, I informed her that if we were shopping at a store that had toys, I would be good. But if we were shopping for ladies' dresses, I would be bad. When you are a six-year-old boy, going dress shopping with your mom is suffering. It's hard to be patient when you're six and surrounded by racks and racks of dresses!

Understanding what makes us impatient isn't our problem. It's cultivating patience that is the issue. Like Mark Twain said, "It ain't those parts of the Bible that I can't understand that bother me, it is the parts that I do understand!"

The kind of patience Paul has in mind when he describes love is being patient with people.

Philip Ryken says patience is having "the ability to put up with the frustrations we will face any time we have a relationship with someone who is just as flawed and every bit as fallen as we are."[6]

So let's do a little self-diagnosis. Take a minute and think carefully about how you would answer these questions. And then think about how your spouse might answer them.

- Are you easily provoked?
- Do your find yourself annoyed or angry when things don't go your way?
- Are there things your spouse does that are triggers for you? What are they?
- When you are inconvenienced, do you become irritated?

- Would your spouse say you can be demanding? In what areas?
- What do you resent about your spouse?
- Can you think of things you do that cause your spouse to become impatient or annoyed with you?
- Are there things your spouse does that cause you to become anxious or nervous?
- Are there times when you find your muscles tightening, or your jaw or fists clench?

There are clearly times when each of us becomes impatient. So is there a cure? An antidote? Is there a way to cultivate patience?

There is. But it's probably not the cure you're imagining.

The antidote for impatience is not "try harder to be a more patient person." It is not "take deep breaths and count to ten." Those are behavior modification techniques that may help you be more patient in the moment, but won't get to the root of the issue.

The way we cultivate patience (or any of the fruit of the Spirit) is first to learn to think about your life and your circumstances from a different perspective. You need to think about your life and what you are experiencing from God's perspective instead of from your perspective.

John Sanderson says the reason impatience is such a noxious weed is because it leaves God out of our thinking.[7] And he's right. It's when we lose sight of God and what he is doing in our lives and in our world that we become impatient. It's when we fail to rest in the cradle of providence that we become agitated.

The first step in cultivating patience is to pause, be still, and ask ourselves the question: "What might God be up to in this moment?"

What if your spouse is doing something that drives you crazy? What if he or she doesn't think clearly and soberly about things (like you think you do)? What if they don't pull their own weight? Or they mess up—regularly? From your perspective, all you see is insensitivity. If your spouse really cared about you, they would simply adjust their behavior.

But how does this situation look from God's perspective?

First, God is in control of everything that is going on, right? God is not looking at your situation and thinking, "I never should have let this happen. I just wasn't paying attention!"

Second, God has placed you in that situation as an ambassador of grace. As his representative. As a missionary. You are there to serve him, not to serve your own agenda.

Third, God cares more about your spouse than he does about tasks. The person who is driving you crazy is someone he created in his own image. Someone he loves. Someone with a soul. Someone in need of grace. And that's why you're there. To act as an agent of grace to your husband or your wife.

Fourth, when you are in a situation where you are inconvenienced or you are called on to suffer, you need to remember that your suffering is part of God's design for your good and for his glory.

The fact that we go through seasons of suffering does not mean that God is not good or that he doesn't love us. God works in the midst of suffering. He is working to conform us to his image. He is working his plan. And his plan is to take us through seasons of suffering in our lives. It's in these seasons that we grow.

Someone has said, "If you knew all that God knows, and you could see all that God can see, you would do exactly what God is doing at this moment in your life."[8]

Or as the old hymn expresses it:

> Farther along we'll know more about it,
> Farther along we'll understand why;
> Cheer up, my brother, live in the sunshine,
> We'll understand it all by and by.[9]

So in every situation, if we can pause and remember that God is in control, God is at work, and there are bigger issues at play, we can begin to rest and find peace and contentment. We can be patient.

Patience is grace fueled by love. We remember that God is patient with us. And we extend that same kind of grace to our spouse when he or she sins against us. When we apply the kind of love the apostle Paul describes in 1 Corinthians 13 to our marriage, our relationship will be marked by a foundational commitment to serving our spouse and helping him or her grow in godliness. It's a commitment that doesn't crumble in the face of adversity or trials. It's a love that says, "My goal is your good, even if it costs me."

Love is patient with others. Love suffers long. Love doesn't lose faith that God is at work.

Talk Together

1. If leaving God out of our thinking tends to make us more impatient, how does keeping God in the forefront of our thinking make us more patient?

2. Whether you are currently married or not, what are the situations in your life right now that God is using to cultivate patience?

CHAPTER 3

The Thing That Is Better Than Life Itself: Love Is Kind

Love is kind.
(1 Cor. 13:4a)

*W*hen love is present in marriage, both spouses will be inclined toward active goodness for one another. My goal = your good.

If the names Wilbur and Charlotte don't immediately ring a bell for you, you should stop reading this immediately and head straight to your local library or to Amazon and obtain a copy of the best-selling children's paperback of all time. With 45 million copies in print in twenty-three languages, it shouldn't be hard for you to get your hands on a copy of the Newbery Award–winning children's book *Charlotte's Web.*

Unless you have young children, it's probably been a few years since you've read *Charlotte's Web.* But if you want to learn something about kindness, it's time to dust off a copy of the E. B. White classic and revisit the story of Zuckerman's Famous Pig.

For those who need their memory jogged, here are the CliffsNotes. Wilbur the pig was the runt of the litter and was spared the farmer's axe through the petitions of his daughter, Fern. She adopted and named the piglet and treated him as her pet. When he became too big for Fern to care for, Wilbur was shipped off to Uncle Homer's barn to await his eventual demise.

The heroine of the story is Charlotte the spider, whose web is spun in the corner of the barn where she can watch all that happens with Wilbur. Charlotte befriends the pig and determines that she must come to his aid. She must find a way to prevent his impending execution.

Charlotte's plan involves writing words in her web, beginning with the declaration, "some pig." The words *terrific, radiant,* and *humble* soon follow. When Uncle Homer spots Charlotte's web artistry, Wilbur becomes a local celebrity and the eventual winner of a special prize at the county fair.

Charlotte's handiwork leads to a stay of execution for Wilbur. But between web-spinning and producing her egg sac, Charlotte soon realizes that her own days are numbered. She breaks the news to Wilbur: she does not have long to live.

Wilbur is distraught, unable to imagine life without Charlotte's friendship. "Why did you do all this for me?" he asks her. "I've never done anything for you."

"You have been my friend." The spider replies: "That in itself is a tremendous thing. I wove my webs for you because I liked you. After all, what's a life, anyway? We're born, we live a little while, we die. A spider's life can't help being something of a mess, with all this trapping and eating flies. By helping you, perhaps I was trying to lift up my life a trifle. Heaven knows anyone's life can stand a little of that."[1]

Anyone who has ever read *Charlotte's Web* recognizes the great irony that the self-sacrificing protagonist is a spider, an insect most of us find both frightening and loathsome. And don't miss the fact that the object of her kindness is a pig, and the runt of the litter at that.

I don't know if E. B. White had ever read the Gospel of John before writing his award-winning story, but *Charlotte's Web* is a parable that illustrates clearly Jesus' words in John 15:13: "Greater love has no one than this, that someone lay down his life for his friends."

The kindness that Charlotte personifies is the kind of life-giving loving-kindness that ought to undergird every marriage. The absence of loving-kindness from a marriage will turn a garden into a desert.

"Be kind to one another," the apostle Paul tells the Ephesians. Be "tenderhearted" (Eph. 4:32).

So what exactly is kindness?

Pastor Tim Keller describes it as "a sincere desire for the happiness of others."[2] Alexander Strauch takes the idea further. He says kindness is "a readiness to do good, to help, to relieve burdens, to be useful, to serve, to be tender and to be sympathetic toward others. It has been said, 'Kindness is love in work clothes.'"[3]

Read that last paragraph again and ask yourself: "Does that sound like me?"

- Would my spouse say I have a sincere desire for his or her happiness? That I am ready to do good? To help?
- What is something I can point to recently that shows my active engagement in attempting to relieve my spouse's burdens?
- Would my spouse say I am a tender and sympathetic person?
- How do I seek to serve my spouse in our marriage?

Author Jerry Bridges says, "Apart from God's grace, most of us naturally tend to be concerned about our responsibilities, our problems, our plans. But the person who has grown in the grace of kindness has expanded his thinking outside of himself and his interests and has developed a genuine interest in the happiness and well-being of those around him."[4]

Just how truly Charlotte-like are you in your marriage?

Most of the time in marriage, we settle into routine and mundane ways of showing kindness to one another. One way we serve each other is by taking care of those household duties that come to all of us. My wife likes doing laundry and cutting the front yard. I stay on top of our finances and handle our tax returns each year. We take turns on gathering the trash and the recycling. We don't stop to thank each other for these repetitive ways of serving one another, but each is an act of kindness as we actively serve one another with joy and without any resentment.

At a marriage conference years ago, Mary Ann and I heard a husband explain that he assumes the responsibility for keeping both of their cars filled with gas so that his wife rarely if ever has to do the pumping on her own. I asked Mary Ann if that was something she'd like for me to do regularly, and she smiled. Since then, I've made it my aim to pay attention to her gas gauge so she doesn't have to worry about it.

I think we should occasionally pause to think about and acknowledge the small acts of kindness we are already doing for one another. When my closet is refreshed with clean clothes, I try to remember to thank my wife for serving me. She often thanks me when I've taken her car to have the oil changed and the tires rotated.

Author Ann Voskamp, in a *FamilyLife Today* radio interview, related a story about simple acts of kindness in her marriage.

> I came out of the back of the house, and he had a ladder up against the house—he's up there working on the eaves. I said to him, "Hon, what are you doing up there?" He turned to me and said, "I'm loving you."
>
> I think, so often, we think love is something *big* that we do—(but) love is all of these little things that we do. We don't have to-do lists; we have to-love lists. It's all these little moments.
>
> Sometimes, we think romance is something Hollywood-like that we do for each other. Really, it's all of those everyday single moments, where we live broken and given—like bread to each other—that sustains relationships in marriages and families.[5]

Talk Together

1. Think of three ways your spouse regularly demonstrates kindness—"love in work clothes"—in your marriage. Thank your spouse for these too-often unacknowledged and unappreciated acts of kindness.

2. Ask your spouse if there is one new habit or practice you could develop that would demonstrate love and kindness. Find delight in expressing love for your mate by serving him or her in this way.

New Testament scholars tell us that the Greek word that is translated "kindness" in our Bibles is an interesting word. It appears that the apostle Paul made it up. He took the Greek noun *chrestos* and turned it into a verb, just like we've done in our day with the proper noun Google—we now Google things.

Chrestos is translated a variety of ways in the Bible: easy, better, good, gracious and kind. Everywhere the word is found, in all of Greek literature, it's always a noun.

Except in the Bible. Right here in 1 Corinthians 13. By turning *chrestos* into a verb, Paul puts kindness in motion. He says this is how kindness acts and what kindness does. Kindness makes things easier and better. Kindness extends grace. That's what *chrestos* does.

We often think of kindness as something small or minor, a social grace. In our mind, kindness involves a mixture of good manners and mostly inconsequential acts of service. We are kind when we open the door for someone or let a person with three items go ahead of us in the checkout line at the grocery store. If you leave a generous tip or offer someone else your seat on the subway, you have demonstrated kindness.

But the biblical idea of kindness is much bigger. A kind person is someone who seeks to actively and lavishly bless another person.

Jesus' entire ministry was marked by kindness toward those in need—the poor, the sick, the outcast, all who would humble themselves and acknowledge their need. He was proactively kind toward the paralytic whose friends lowered him down through the roof. He was kind toward the centurion whose daughter had died. He was kind toward the widow at Nain whose son had died.

Want another example of what real kindness looks like? Consider how it is described for us in Titus 3: "We ourselves were once foolish, disobedient, led astray, slaves to various passions and pleasures, passing our days in malice and envy, hated by others and hating one another" (v. 3).

That's not a particularly flattering description, is it? Paul does not pull punches. Instead of describing us as good-hearted people with a few rough edges, he makes sure we don't gloss over the reality of our sinful condition. He tells it like it is.

Now think honestly for a second. If your spouse lived out that description on a daily basis—if he or she was foolish, or disobedient, a slave to passions and pleasures, full of envy, malice and hatred—how would you be predisposed to acting toward him or her? You might start out intending to be patient and kind, but that probably wouldn't last long.

But look at what the Bible says about how God responds to our sinful nature:

> But when the *goodness and loving kindness of God* our Savior appeared, he saved us, not because of works done by us in righteousness, but according to his own mercy, by the washing of regeneration and renewal of the Holy Spirit, whom he poured out on us richly through Jesus Christ our Savior, so that being justified by his grace we might become heirs according to the hope of eternal life. (Titus 3:4–7, emphasis added)

God's response to our sinful, self-absorbed nature is goodness and loving-kindness. Imagine. "It seems," says author Jerry Bridges, "the Bible goes out of its way to portray the kindness of God in stark contrast to man's total undeservedness."[6]

God's kindness has a softening effect on our stubborn, hard hearts. It leads us to repentance (Rom. 2:4). And God demonstrates his love for us in a supreme act of kindness. While we were still rebelling against him, Jesus died for us (Rom. 5:8).

Our sinful condition is no small matter. And neither is God's loving-kindness.

Now think for a minute about the Old Testament. God's loving-kindness is spoken of over and over again, more than 250 times. It's how we translate the Hebrew word *hesed*. That word is used more often in the Old Testament to describe God's character than any other single word. The writers of the Old Testament were apparently struck by the loving-kindness of God toward his stubborn and rebellious children.

"The great surprise of the Hebrew Bible," says author and songwriter Michael Card, "is not that God is awesome or holy. These are characteristics we would expect from God. The great surprise is that he is kind, that he is a God of *hesed*."[7]

The Bible describes God's loving-kindness as abundant (Isa. 63:7) and everlasting (Isa. 54:8). God abounds in loving-kindness (Neh. 9:17). This is not a quality that was characteristic of the pagan deities. The idea that Yahweh, the omnipotent, creator God, also abounds in loving-kindness was something that caused the Israelites to marvel. In fact, King David went so far as to declare that God's loving-kindness is "better than life" (Ps. 63:3).

God's kindness toward us is big. It's powerful. It's the active expression of his great love for us.

And our kindness toward each other in marriage is powerful as well. As we grow in this grace, and as this fruit of the Spirit becomes more a part of our transformed character, our love for one another takes on a new, deeper dimension. God's kindness toward us softens our hard hearts. Our kindness toward one another can have the same effect.

Talk Together

1. Make a list of at least five ways God has demonstrated his kindness toward you. Think of specific, practical matters. Share your list with your spouse or your fiancé.

2. Can you think of a time when someone has been kind to you and it has softened your heart toward him or her? Share the experience with your spouse.

Kindness acts like a marital disinfectant, cleaning away the corrosive buildup that can weaken a marriage.

But kindness doesn't come naturally. We have to teach two-year-olds to be kind toward others. Kindness is a fruit of the Spirit, not a function of our flesh. It's not our nature to be warm or generous, thoughtful or helpful toward others—to actively seek someone else's good.

Lewis Smedes says kindness is being ready to enhance the life of another person. It "is enormous strength—more than most of us have, except now and then. . . . Kindness is the power that moves us to support and heal someone who offers nothing in return. Kindness is the power to move a self-centered ego toward the weak, the ugly, the hurt, and to move that ego to invest itself in personal care with no expectation of reward."[8]

The early Church Father John Chrysostom said that kindness goes beyond nobly enduring a wrong. It goes beyond serving or comforting the one who wronged you. Kindness, he says, is seeking to cure the sore and heal the wound of a broken relationship.[9]

In other words, kindness is not a sentimental feeling we have. It's a rugged demonstration of our active love for another person.

We sometimes let ourselves off the hook when it comes to kindness. We say, "It's the thought that counts." But that's not really true. We can think kind things about our spouse, but until we act kindly toward him or her, we haven't really loved him or her yet.

Where does this kind of love come from? How do we cultivate kindness in our marriage?

Remember the Greek word *chrestos*? The noun that the apostle Paul turned into a verb? That word became the identifying label for the first Christians. The ancient historian Tertullian says that in the early days of the church, Christians were sometimes called *Chres-tiani*, instead of *Christ-iani*. It was a play on words. The "Christ ones" were the kind ones.[10]

They were no different than us. They were not somehow more naturally predisposed than we are to be kind to others. So how did kindness become an identifying characteristic for them?

The same way it will for us. Kindness grows in our hearts as we meditate on the remarkable kindness of God demonstrated by the sacrifice of Jesus for us. As you think about how God has lavished kindness on you, God will stir in you a desire to become a channel of God's kindness toward others. The crucifixion of Jesus is the most profound demonstration of God's loving-kindness in all of history. And the more we consider it, the more we think about it, the more it begins to reform our own way of thinking and acting toward others.

As a practical matter, C. S. Lewis said that the way to cultivate kindness—or any of the characteristics of godly love—is to decide to do kind things whether we feel like it or not.

> Do not waste time bothering whether you "love" your neighbor; act as if you did. As soon as we do this we find one of the great secrets. When you are behaving as if you loved someone, you will presently come to love him. . . . Do not sit trying to manufacture feelings. Ask yourself, "If I were sure that I loved God, what would I do?" When you have found the answer, go and do it.[11]

If kindness is missing from your marriage, the first step in growing in grace is to confess to God that your lack of kindness is a sin against him. Don't make excuses for yourself. Don't try to justify your hard-heartedness. An absence of kindness in our lives reflects a lack of godliness. An unkind Christian is an oxymoron. We're not following Jesus when we aren't being kind.

Once you've confessed that your lack of kindness is a sin, take time to study and meditate on the kindness of God for you. Go to a website like Bible Gateway or ESVBible.org and do a word search for "kindness." Read the passages that describe kindness. Take time to think deeply about all the ways God has demonstrated kindness toward you.

And as you do, ask God to fill you with his Spirit, to empower you to respond with kindness toward others even when you're not feeling it. Come up with a list of ways you can proactively demonstrate kindness toward your spouse. Your list will include specific actions you can begin to implement that can grow to become regular habits of kindness. It will include how you communicate with your spouse, giving focused attention as you engage with each other and as you learn to control a critical or harsh tongue. And it will involve acts of service you can perform that can help make your spouse's load lighter and not heavier.

Kindness can seem like such a small thing. But researchers who have studied the differences between marriages that thrive and marriages that struggle have come to this conclusion: the amount of kindness expressed in marriage is the single greatest predictor of marital satisfaction and stability. It's the glue that holds couples together.

CHAPTER 4

It's Not All about Me:
Love Is Humble

Love does not envy or boast;
it is not arrogant.
(1 Cor. 13:4)

hen I look back on my motivations for marriage as a twenty-three-year-old, it's easy for me to spot the faulty view of love that was driving me to the altar.

I was in love with how I felt being with someone who thought I was special. I was in love with the idea of spending the rest of my life with someone who would be devoted to reminding me regularly just how special I was.

There might be a kernel of truth to the old joke about the woman who, when she was asked about the secret to her marital success, replied, "We're both in love with the same person."

Of course, those were clearly not my conscious thoughts. I knew marriage was more about giving than getting. I knew it would require sacrifice. And I was happy to sacrifice . . . as long as Mary Ann kept her part of the bargain and kept me at the center of her world.

Most of us have learned over the years how to keep our inherent narcissism concealed. It's clear to us how unattractive self-love is, so we do all we can to try to mask our vanity.

But at our core, our default setting is arrogance. We are infected with what the Bible calls "the boastful pride of life" (1 John 2:16 NASB). Arrogance and self-love are the opposite of authentic love. They are the antithesis of what Paul is describing in 1 Corinthians 13. And when we fail to recognize and address our essential self-centeredness, the toxic gasses of arrogance begin to poison our relationships.

The word that is translated "arrogant" in 1 Corinthians 13 is a word Paul has already used several times in this letter. Interestingly, it's a word that appears only seven times in the New Testament, and six of those times are in 1 Corinthians.

The church members in Corinth had a pride problem. They had an inflated opinion of their own wisdom and giftedness. They had a puffed-up view of themselves.

J. B. Phillips in his paraphrase of 1 Corinthians 13 says, "Love does not cherish inflated ideas of its own importance." That's a good picture of arrogance. It is a sinful, self-focused response to the successes we experience in life. Instead of recognizing the contribution of others to any success we have experienced, we see ourselves as "self-made." We take all the glory for ourselves. And instead of realizing that every good and perfect gift comes from the hand of God, we naturally rob God of his glory and take it all for ourselves.

Writing to the church at Rome, Paul said, "For by the grace given to me I say to everyone among you not to think of himself more highly than he ought to think, but to think with sober judgment, each according to the measure of faith that God has assigned" (Rom. 12:3). And in the same chapter, he said, "Do not be haughty, but associate with the lowly. Never be wise in your own sight" (v. 16).

If arrogance is having an inflated opinion of yourself, boasting is letting others know about that opinion. We crave the admiration of others. We long for recognition and significance. So we look for socially acceptable ways to say, "Look at me."

The rise in popularity of social media has brought with it what is now referred to as the *humblebrag*. In fact, the word has even found its way into the *Merriam Webster* online dictionary, where it is defined as making "a seemingly modest, self-critical, or casual statement or reference that is meant to draw attention to one's admirable or impressive qualities or achievements."[1]

The Urban Dictionary defines it this way: A *humblebrag* is "when you, usually consciously, try to get away with bragging about yourself by couching it in a phony show of humility."[2] Examples include: "I'm exhausted from my two-week vacation in Hawaii! I need a vacation!" Or "I'm really ticked that I wasn't able to improve my bench max past 220 this week!"

Or a humblebrag might sound like this.

I had recently filled up Mary Ann's car with gas, but she had not noticed or acknowledged my amazing act of sacrificial service. So while she was driving, I casually asked her, "Does your car need gas?"

I knew it didn't need gas! I was really saying, "Don't you see what a great guy I am? And why haven't you said so recently?"

When we bring an inflated sense of our importance into our marriage and insist that our spouse acknowledge how wonderful we are, we're about as far from love as we can get. Love is about pouring ourselves out for others. Arrogance is about insisting that others pour out praise and admiration for us. And bragging about ourselves is just a verbal billboard that declares how insecure we really are.

"It is impossible to love and to boast at the same time," says Philip Ryken, "because when we boast, we demand the center stage, whereas love shines the spotlight of its affection on one of the other actors in the drama of life."[3]

In marriage, arrogance says, "I'm what is most important here. It's your job to make me feel loved, and I'll be the judge of how you're doing!" But the kind of love being described in 1 Corinthians 13 says, "I'm committed to your good. I'm willing to sacrifice for you because you matter to me. I want you to know how important I think you are."

With real love, self is not ignored. But it takes a back seat to helping your spouse flourish.

Talk Together

1. Identify and share with your spouse one self-centered motivation you had for getting married.

2. What is one area of your life where you think you don't get the recognition or respect you deserve? How are you sometimes tempted to want to draw attention to yourself in that area?

Since it was published in 1992, Gary Chapman's book *The Five Love Languages* has helped millions of couples—including Mary Ann and me—better understand how we can more effectively communicate our love for each other. Chapman lists five common ways we express love: (1) words of affirmation, (2) quality time, (3) giving gifts, (4) acts of service, and (5) physical touch. He says that all of us feel loved in different ways, and we most commonly express our love for one another in the same way that we most often feel loved. We need to learn our spouse's love language, Chapman says, so we can communicate our affection and appreciation for them in the way that speaks love to them.

Words of affirmation would be at the top of my love language list. I like it when people notice and affirm and praise me. If I'm honest, I care most about words of affirmation if they're coming from people whose opinion I respect! In fact, there have been a handful of unforgettable affirming statements that people for whom I have great respect have shared with me over the years. Those words of praise are etched deeply in my psyche.

As a freshman in college, I tried out for an on-air shift at the college radio station. I'm convinced the station had no listeners. But on Tuesday nights from 9:00 p.m. until 1:00 a.m., it didn't matter to me. I was living the dream of being a disc jockey!

I'd been on air for a few months when I ran into the station manager, a professor at the university who oversaw the operation of the station. He asked me my name and seemed to be aware of my Tuesday night shift. "Where did you work before you worked here?" he asked me. I told him this was my first radio job. "Really?" he said. "You sound good."

I can take you today to the spot inside the station where that conversation took place. I can still hear those words of affirmation ringing in my ears more than forty years later.

Jump ahead twenty-five years. I had just finished speaking to a small group, giving a message about the need for the fruit of the Holy Spirit to define who we are as followers of Jesus. After the message was over, I had a seminary professor who had been in the audience pull me aside and say to me "that was the finest message on the fruit of the Spirit I have ever heard."

Once again, those words of encouragement are still stamped on my soul.

We all need cheerleaders in our lives. We need the boost that comes from affirming words. Not flattery. Not empty praise. But solid encouragement that comes when our gifts and abilities are recognized and affirmed. No one wants to feed pride and arrogance. The Bible tells us to speak words to each other that are "good for building up," words that "give grace to those who hear" (Eph. 4:29). We are to "encourage one another and build one another up" (1 Thess. 5:11). A marriage won't thrive without a husband and wife offering enthusiastic encouragement for one another.

But there's a dark side that can accompany our desire for words of affirmation. In fact, after my seminary professor friend praised my message on the fruit of the Spirit, I remember wanting to find some way to share his praise with others. Hearing his encouragement wasn't enough for me; I wanted everyone to know how good he thought my message had been!

If, like me, words of affirmation is at the top of your love language list, it's probably worth considering whether there is something inside of you that is driving your need for affirmation. We all like being encouraged. But what happens if we have an unhealthy need to be honored or praised? How does that work out in a marriage? Could our arrogance and bragging reflect how we, in our own insecurity, are attempting to draw attention to ourselves and to seek the approval and praise of people—including our spouse—instead of living our lives for God's approval?

When arrogance or boasting are part of a marriage relationship, the puffed-up focus will drain the life and love from the union.

If your spouse is arrogant, offering words of affirmation can feel like feeding the monster. To praise someone who already thinks more highly of himself than he ought seems counterintuitive. Instead, we can feel like maybe we ought to knock the guy down a few rungs.

This is where it's important to understand the difference between encouragement and flattery. Flattery is designed to appeal to someone's ego, usually for the purpose of manipulation. But encouraging and building up our spouse is part of our assignment in marriage.

I love how my friend Robyn McKelvy explains it. Robyn was a cheerleader in high school. The word she uses to describe the team she cheered for is "stinky." But the team's performance did not keep her and her fellow cheerleaders from cheering for them.

She sees parallels in marriage. She tells wives, "The day you put on your wedding dress, you put on a new cheerleader outfit."[4] And I should note: the same goes for husbands. Guys, you are your wife's number-one cheerleader. You both cheer for each other in marriage even when the team is losing. Cheering, when done right, doesn't enable arrogance; it offers encouragement and support.

I spent more than a quarter of a century working with Dennis Rainey, the founder and president of FamilyLife. As a daily radio host, bestselling author, sought-after speaker, and ministry leader, Dennis has been used by God to touch millions of people's lives and marriages. I know people who are still married today because of the wisdom and guidance they received from Dennis's speaking and writing.

I heard Dennis say many times that what fueled his effectiveness in ministry was his wife's encouragement. "She believed in me more than I believed in myself. She kept me going. She cheered me on. Her affirmation was the wind beneath my wings."[5]

Would your spouse say you offer enthusiastic encouragement? Or are you stingy with words of praise because you fear your applause will cause your spouse to think too highly of himself or herself? That cheering them on will somehow go to their head?

Remember what the Proverbs say. "Death and life are in the power of the tongue" (Prov. 18:21). "A word fitly spoken is like apples of gold in a setting of silver" (Prov. 25:11). Helping your spouse remain humble doesn't mean you never encourage or affirm or cheer for him or her.

Talk Together

1. How important to you are words of affirmation from your spouse? Is too much of your identity built around his or her affirmation? What happens if your spouse doesn't affirm you?

2. Think about the line between words of affirmation and flattery. Especially if you aren't yet married, but would like to be, how can you speak words of encouragement to your someone special without crossing over into flattery?

Ultimately it's up to each one of us to address the arrogance and pride in our lives. To do that, we'll have to explore what the Bible teaches about humility and how to pursue it.

I think a lot of people are confused about humility. If arrogance is having an inflated opinion of yourself, then someone might conclude that humility is the opposite—having a low opinion of yourself. Humble people, they assume, are people who dismiss praise and downplay any acclaim. People who don't believe their own press.

But humility isn't some kind of false modesty. Humility isn't about not having a low self assessment, but a correct self-assessment. That means we understand our gifts and abilities. And we understand where those gifts and abilities come from.

We understand that each one of us has value, worth, and dignity as image-bearers of God.

At the same time, we understand clearly the reality of our fallen nature. We understand that when Romans 3:10 says "there is no one righteous, not even one," we are included in that description.

The Bible ensures that we don't think too highly of ourselves, or too lowly of ourselves. God wants us to have a correct self-appraisal—to understand what is true about our worth and value, and at the same time to understand what is true about our sinful nature. The more we come to understand these things, the more that understanding will produce humility in us.

When we understand and see ourselves as we truly are, as the Bible describes our condition, there is no way to remain arrogant. Even in areas where we may excel in comparison to others, we have to recognize that the gifts and abilities we have come from the God who created us, shaped us, and ordered every aspect of our lives.

The apostle Paul makes this point in 1 Corinthians 4:7 when he says to the Corinthians, "What do you have that you did not receive? If then you received it, why do you boast as if you did not receive it?"

According to the great eighteenth-century pastor and theologian Jonathan Edwards, "True humility cannot exist unless the creature feels his distance from God, not only in respect to his greatness, but also to his loveliness."[6] In other words, no matter how great or lovely you are, God is infinitely greater and lovelier than you.

We can see how this understanding of God's character and our sinfulness can produce humility. But how does humility cause us to be more loving? By directing our focus away from ourselves. The more attention you pay to self, the less attention you are paying to God or to other people. The less attention you are paying to self, the more capacity you have to pay attention to the needs of others.

Talk Together

1. Read Mark 7:21–23. Do these verses describe a certain group of people or all humans? To what extent do they describe you?

2. If pride is the natural state of humans, what is our only hope? How can we be changed?

The goal in marriage is oneness. That's God's plan and his design for us. He takes two people—a man and a woman—and tells them to leave their fathers and mothers and to hold fast to one another. And as they do, the two become one.

Oneness will never happen in a marriage without humility. Boasting and arrogance are the enemies of oneness.

The opposite of oneness is autonomy and independence. It's isolation. The by-product of autonomy and isolation is loneliness.

At each stage of creation, as God completed his work, he looked at what he had done and declared, "It is good." That is, until we get to the middle of Genesis 2. It's there that God looks at his handiwork and says, "Something is not good here. It's incomplete. It's unfinished. I still have some work to do."

"It is not good for the man to be alone," God said. "I will make a helper suitable for him" (v. 18 NIV).

God made us to be social creatures. We need relationships. And marriage is God's good gift to us to address our aloneness need and to give us a living picture of his relationship with us.

For those whom God has given the gift of singleness, he provides other channels for the aloneness need to be met. The church is a primary channel. Singles need deep spiritual friendships to thrive.

But for most of us, a primary way God addresses our aloneness need is in marriage. He takes two and makes them one.

If you're wondering how all this ties into arrogance and boasting, stay with me.

One of the places in Scripture where God gives us a description of oneness in relationships is at the beginning of Philippians 2. Although the context is not marriage, the picture of oneness drawn for us in this text helps us understand what marital oneness should look like.

> So if there is any encouragement in Christ, any comfort from love, any participation in the Spirit, any affection and sympathy, complete my joy by being of the same mind, having the same love, being in full accord and of one mind. (Phil. 2:1–2)

The Bible is not talking about sameness when it talks about oneness. Unity and oneness involve bringing together different people with different gifts and different ideas about how life should be done and uniting them around a set of common convictions or beliefs that transcend those differences. Unity comes when what unites a couple is more important than their differences.

One Bible translation describes unity as two or more people who are "intent on one purpose." Pastor and author Kent Hughes says what the Bible is describing is not some kind of "a vacuous togetherness but a oneness fraught with dynamic purpose."[7]

So how do we cultivate oneness in marriage? Philippians 2 gives us a road map. To get there, we have to cultivate a self-emptying humility. We have to learn how to declare war on our pride and self-centeredness.

Oneness and pride will not mix. That's why, as the Bible addresses the goal of oneness, it maps out in very practical terms what it takes to move a relationship in that direction.

> Do nothing from selfish ambition or conceit,
> but in humility count others more significant
> than yourselves. Let each of you look not only
> to his own interests, but also to the interests of
> others. (Phil. 2:3–4)

As I have spoken to and listened to married couples for more than a quarter of a century, I've come to the conclusion that if we could learn to apply those two verses consistently, most of the difficulties we experience in marriage would evaporate. Humility is the foundation of oneness.

Paul is not proposing a false view of humility that thinks other people are better than we are. He is saying that we should regard the needs of others as higher than our own.

In fact, real love doesn't begin until someone else's needs are more important than your own. And as we've already seen, Jesus said it this way: "Greater love has no one than this, that someone lay down his life for his friends" (John 15:13).

Think about the implications for marriage of those first four verses in Philippians 2. Read through them again slowly and prayerfully, phrase by phrase. Think about how radically different your marriage would be if both of you were actively pursuing oneness and at the same time actively regarding one another as more important than yourself.

Does that describe you? Would others say about you that you regularly put the needs of others ahead of your own? Would your spouse and your children say they know they are loved because you lay down your life for them?

Let me add an important disclaimer here. Putting the needs of others ahead of your own needs is not the same as catering to the whims of your spouse. There is a difference between humbly serving each other and accommodating sinfulness or selfishness. Enabling or choosing not to confront ongoing sinful behavior in your spouse is not loving. (We've already addressed this to some extent in chapter 2.) Laying down your life for your spouse sometimes means confronting destructive activities or behaviors.

As you seek to serve your spouse, how you serve should be based on what is best for him or her in the long run, not necessarily what will make him or her happy in the moment. Being humble doesn't mean the other person always gets what he or she wants. It means you put their needs ahead of your own.

Ligon Duncan, the chancellor of Reformed Theological Seminary says that humility is the key to joy in marriage and in all of our relationships.

> The key to a life of joy (the kind of joy that Paul is talking about—not superficial joy, not trivial joy, not joy in sunsets, not joy in wife, not joy in children, not joy in cars, not joy in football, not joy in money, not joy in beauty, not joy in esteem, not joy in influence, not joy in anything else this world can give, but joy in Christ) . . . the key to a life of joy is . . . *a God-centered, gospel-based, grace-enabled shifting of our attention away from ourselves and onto others.* (emphasis added)[8]

When we experience disunity or discord in our marriage, here are the questions we need to ask ourselves:

- Do we really understand and believe the gospel?
- Do we comprehend all God has done for us in Christ?
- Do we understand his love for us? His grace poured out on us? His mercy and his compassion?

The sure cure for arrogance is to refocus our hearts on the remarkable humility that Jesus demonstrates in the gospel.

There is no seven-step plan that eliminates arrogance. There is no quick fix for a heart prone to responding rudely to others. A work of God's grace is required for these stubborn habits to begin to fade in us. By his Spirit and through the power of his Word, God will do a work of grace in our hearts as we humble ourselves before him and as we regularly take time to consider again what Jesus has done for us in his death and resurrection.

Isaac Watts understood this well. He wrote about the work God does in our hearts when we take time to reflect again on the gospel.

> When I survey the wondrous cross
> On which the Prince of glory died,
> My richest gain I count but loss,
> And pour contempt on all my pride.[9]

It's hard to hold on to arrogance and to think of ourselves as more important than others when we spend time thinking about the Son of God hanging on a cross for us.

Talk Together

1. Read the words of the hymn "When I Survey the Wondrous Cross" by Isaac Watts. Have you experienced how the cross rids us of arrogance and pride?

2. Why do you think it's so hard for us to consider others' needs before our own even though we know what Christ did for us?

So how do we humble ourselves? Simply put, we remind ourselves of just who God is and who we are. We recognize that all we have in life is a gift from him. We teach our soul to boast in him, not in ourselves (Ps. 34:2). We put into action the words of Jeremiah 9:

> Let not the wise man boast in his wisdom, let not the mighty man boast in his might, let not the rich man boast in his riches, but let him who boasts boast in this, that he understands and knows me, that I am the LORD who practices steadfast love, justice, and righteousness in the earth. For in these things I delight, declares the LORD. (vv. 23–24)

Humility is ultimately expressed in surrender. In letting go. In giving up. We cast our cares on him. We cry out. We confess again our total dependence on him. And when we need God to pour his grace into our soul, we humbly ask him. He gives grace to the humble.

In marriage, we will face ongoing battles with our passions and desires that will lead to fights and wars (James 4:1–2). Whenever we find ourselves in conflict, we need to remind ourselves that we are not wrestling against flesh and blood; we're in a spiritual battle (Eph. 6:12). Our spouse in not our enemy. And in every spiritual battle we face, the solution is the same. We humble ourselves before God, because he resists the proud, but gives grace to the humble (James 4:6).

When a husband and wife are humble-hearted and are committed to putting the needs of one another ahead of their own needs, discord and strife and division will not survive. They will melt away.

"Do nothing from selfish ambition or conceit, but in humility count others more significant than yourselves" (Phil. 2:3).

Talk Together

1. Think of an example of how your spouse or your intended has placed your needs above his or her own. Which of you would you say most often demonstrates this kind of humility in your relationship?

2. Read again what Ligon Duncan describes as "the key to a life of joy: *a God-centered, gospel-based, grace-enabled shifting of our attention away from ourselves and onto others.*" If you took the first step, what impact might a shift like this have in your relationship with one another?

CHAPTER 5

It's My Way or the Love Way: Love Is Generous

It does not insist on its own way.
(1 Cor. 13:5a)

hildren want the things they want, when they want them. I was no exception.

In my elementary school days, the principal at Henry Hough Elementary in Glendale, Missouri, was working on his doctorate in education, and he decided to use my classmates and me as guinea pigs to test his thesis. His doctoral work was exploring how to best teach the basic principles of democracy and civil government to fifth and sixth graders. His working theory was that by reenacting the work of the founding fathers in establishing the US Constitution, fifth and sixth grade students would not only learn American history, they would learn the fundamentals of democracy at the same time.

So, my fellow classmates and I became his control group to test his theory. During the fall of my sixth-grade year, our class held a constitutional convention and elected delegates to write our own set of founding documents. And in the spring, we again held elections, this time deciding who we wanted to serve as class representatives and other elected officials.

I was part of the constitutional convention that was tasked to work on our founding documents. And it did not go well. Our teachers did their best, but we were a room full of eleven- and twelve-year-olds with short attention spans and a lack of clear guidance. Drafting constitutional documents is a difficult task for a group of a dozen adults; it was pretty much impossible for us.

But the job had to be done. And so as we headed into Christmas break, our teacher took one of my classmates and me aside and asked us if the two of us could maybe get together over Christmas break and finish drafting the constitution.

No one likes having homework over Christmas break. But honestly, this assignment was a dream come true for me for two reasons. First, the other student selected for the task just happened to be my sixth-grade crush, Lisa. (Looking back, I have to wonder if my teacher knew that we kind of liked each other and was playing matchmaker!) Because of this assignment, there was now a reason for Lisa and me to spend time together during the break!

The other reason I was looking forward to the task was because I had ambitions. My sights were set on running for and being elected president of my elementary school. And I reasoned that if I could influence the drafting of our constitution, I could have it written in a way that would make life better for me if I won the election.

So Lisa and I got together during the break. And over Campbell's Mushroom Soup and Vernor's Ginger Ale that my grandparents had brought from Michigan for the holidays, we wrote the constitution. Well, actually, I dictated, and Lisa wrote.

Our constitution called for the House of Representatives and the Senate to meet once a week. Believing in a strong working relationship between the legislative and executive branches of government, I determined it would be necessary for the president to be on hand any time either body was in session. So we included in our constitution specific times for those legislative bodies to meet. The House met once a week during a time when I had math class. The Senate met on a different day, during the time I had science. That meant that if I was elected, I would be able to legitimately skip my two least favorite classes every week!

My plan worked. Our constitution was approved. Elections were held and I won. And it all happened without anyone recognizing the self-serving motivations that were at work behind the scenes.

Or maybe someone caught on. Because in the final week of school, my classmates all signed a petition calling for my impeachment.

I still have the document. I'd like to think it was all an affectionate prank. But who knows.

First Corinthians 13:5 is what led me to think about my elementary school days. It's there that the Bible explains that genuine love is not self-seeking. Love does not seek its own, or as the ESV says, love "does not insist on its own way." Eugene Peterson paraphrases the verse this way: "Love isn't always 'me first'" (MSG).

When I was in sixth grade, I was pretty much all in on "me first." My tenure as president of the fifth and sixth grade was all about me and the personal benefit I could receive during my time in office. Come to think of it, maybe our class experiment in civics actually did teach us a few things about real-life government and politics after all . . .

There is a story told of a mom who was making cookies one day. Her two children were in the kitchen with her waiting for the first cookies to come out of the oven, arguing about who would get the first cookie. The mom saw a teaching opportunity here and said to the kids, "You know what Jesus would do if he was here, right? He would say, 'You go first.'"

At which point the older brother said to the younger brother, "You be Jesus."

Somewhere along the way, most of us learned that it's not polite to insist that things be done our way. But when we're honest with ourselves, we know that deep down, every one of us believes there is a right way for things to be done. And that "right way" is most often the way that serves our interests.

Think back to the rebellion in Genesis 3. God had told the man and the woman that they were free to eat of every tree in the garden except one. But when the woman took the bite of the forbidden fruit and gave it to the man who was with her, both of them were declaring to God that they knew best how to serve their interests and needs.

Burger King's breakthrough advertising campaign years ago—the thing that made them different from McDonald's—was that at Burger King you could "have it your way." *We all want it our way.*

Do you know what song, according to *The Guardian* newspaper, is the most often sung song at funerals in Great Britain?

It's a song that singer-songwriter Paul Anka first heard in 1967 (the same year I was writing my own constitution for a government that would serve my needs and my schedule). Anka was vacationing in the South of France when he heard a song performed by a French pop star named Claude François, a song called "Comme d'habitude." He had no idea what the French lyrics were about, but he loved the melody and he flew to Paris to negotiate for the rights to the song.

He was able to get the publishing rights for the song for no cost, while the authors retained the rights to the melody.

A year later, Paul Anka was having dinner in Florida with Frank Sinatra, and Sinatra was not in a very good mood. He told Anka, "I'm quitting the business. I'm sick of it. I'm just getting out."

Later that year, the conversation with Sinatra still ringing in his ears, Anka rewrote the lyrics for the French song he had acquired.

"At one o'clock in the morning," Paul Anka said, "I sat down at an old IBM electric typewriter and said, 'If Frank were writing this about quitting the business, what would he say?' And I started, metaphorically, 'And now the end is near.'"

Anka finished the song at 5:00 a.m. "I called Frank in Nevada—he was at Caesar's Palace—and said, 'I've got something really special for you.'"[1]

Sinatra recorded his version of the song "My Way" on December 30, 1968, and it was released in early 1969. It quickly became one of Sinatra's trademark songs. In fact, in the United Kingdom, the single achieved a still unmatched record, spending seventy-five weeks in the Top 40.[2]

Is "My Way" the song you'd like to have played at your funeral? Is that what you'd like your legacy to be—you did it your way? Is that the statement you'd like to have as the defining statement of your life?

The song is a modern hymn to self-reliance, self-determination, and the triumph of running your own life and calling your own shots. Which, according to the Bible, is exactly what our lives ought not be about.

In a *FamilyLife Today* interview years ago with John Piper, he talked about his own tendency to become impatient and irritable when things aren't going his way. He said when he acted this way at home, his family would sing to him the worship song that includes the line, "It's all about you, Jesus," but they would replace Jesus with Johnny. "It's all about you, Johnny." He said that usually made him more irritable!

The truth is, we are all naturally self-seeking. Each of us is hardwired to want things our way. We want life to be about us, and we want the people around us to conform to our desires and our preferences.

You recognize this tendency in your heart, don't you?

The underlying issue in a lot of marriages today is that we have "my way" husbands and wives trying to turn my way into our way. When marriage is dominated by "my way" thinking, love evaporates quickly.

Talk Together

1. Has there been a time in your life when you have cleverly engineered events to serve your own interests?

2. Can you think of an area in your marriage where the two of you both have strong but opposite feelings about the "right" way to do something? To what extent might your feelings be self-serving?

But aren't there times when it's right for things to go your way? Aren't there times when your way is right and you're in charge and people just need to do what you tell them? In fact, aren't there times you should insist on it?

Sure there are. In business, supervisors have to insist on people doing what they've been told to do. That's true for teachers, for parents, for law enforcement personnel, and for any number of people in positions of authority.

The issue in 1 Corinthians 13 is not an issue of whether it's loving to exercise authority over someone else. It's an issue of a person insisting that things need to be done his way for his benefit.

Where the tendency to become self-seeking often creeps in and begins to erode love in marriage is in areas where decision-making is required. For husbands, self-seeking can easily emerge when we exercise leadership based on our own desires or preferences. For a wife, self-seeking shows up in sometimes subtle and sometimes overt attempts to control her husband or her children.

According to the Bible, there is, by God's design, a defined leadership structure for marriage. It's outlined in 1 Corinthians 11:3: "But I want you to understand that the head of every man is Christ, the head of a wife is her husband, and the head of Christ is God."

Try reading that verse in any setting other than a church and imagine the howls or scowls you'll get. And there are good reasons why. Too many husbands who profess faith in Christ have exercised a kind of "leadership" that lacks love and is unmistakably self-seeking.

But the main reason people don't talk in polite company about a husband being the head of his wife is because we are more interested in fitting into patterns of marriage that are culturally supported than in aligning our lives around God's Word. The idea that a husband is to assume a leadership responsibility in marriage (that he is to love and serve his wife as Christ loves and serves the church) and that his wife is to respect and submit to his leadership (as the church respects and submits to the leadership of Christ) is clearly taught in Scripture. There have been any number of attempts by academics and scholars in our day to use some hermeneutical jujitsu to suggest that the Bible doesn't really teach male leadership in marriage. But these approaches to interpreting the relevant passages of Scripture are a recent historical phenomenon that runs parallel to our culture's rejection of biblical ideas about marriage and gender norms.

In fact, because the steady cultural drumbeat has brought about an erosion of biblical thinking in these critical areas, many people today find the idea of male headship in marriage oppressive and absurd.

The most common objection to the historical understanding of headship and submission in marriage involves the verse in Ephesians 5 that precedes Paul's instructions for married couples. In the context of unpacking what it looks like for a Christian to walk in a manner worthy of his or her calling (Eph. 4:1), Paul explains that we are to live our lives under the influence and control of the Holy Spirit. Each of us is to be "filled with the Spirit," he says (Eph. 5:18).

One of the ways we demonstrate that we are filled with the Spirit is by "submitting to one another out of reverence for Christ." That statement in Ephesians 5:21 is the thesis statement for what follows. A person who is operating under the influence of the Holy Spirit, who is living a Spirit-controlled life, will graciously submit themselves to others who God has placed in authority over them.

Paul shows what submission should look like by pointing to the institution of marriage (Eph. 5:22–33), to parenting (Eph. 6:1–4) and to the workplace (Eph. 6:5–9). In each of these three areas, Paul speaks to both the person who is called upon to lead (husbands, fathers, and masters) as well as the people who are called upon to come under and submit to godly leadership (wives, children, and bondservants). The point Paul is making is that Spirit-led, Spirit-filled people will demonstrate sacrificial servant leadership when they are in positions of authority, and they will model appropriate submission when they are under God-ordained authority.

In other words, when a person in authority becomes a self-seeking and self-serving leader, that person is no longer being led by the Holy Spirit. And when a person refuses to yield to or chafes against godly leadership, that person is walking in the flesh and not in the Spirit.

You may have heard people say that the Bible teaches "mutual submission" in marriage. That's a contradiction. It's an oxymoron. The Greek word translated "submit" is the word *hupotasso*. It was a military term that literally means to arrange under or to subordinate; to subject yourself to another person. It's clear how this works in the military. Privates are led by sergeants, who are led by lieutenants, who are led by captains, and so on. Would mutual submission work in the military? Of course not! Structure and hierarchy are necessary for the military to function effectively.

Why would Paul use a military term like this and apply it to marriage? It's not because he is advocating for husbands to bark orders at their wives like drill sergeants do or for a wife to snap to attention, salute, and say, "Yes, sir," whenever her husband speaks. No, the use of the term is designed to communicate a God-established order in marriage where a husband ultimately bears the weight that goes with "the buck stops here" kind of leadership in his marriage and in his home, and where a wife willingly places herself under her husband's godly leadership.

Those who have presumed that Ephesians 5:21 is a call to some sort of "mutual submission" in marriage are misinterpreting what Paul is saying. They are trying to soften the biblical call to leadership and submission in order to accommodate the spirit of the age. Almost no one who advocates for mutual submission in marriage goes on to suggest that there should be mutual submission between parents and children or between slaves and masters.

When the Bible says we are to submit to one another out of reverence for Christ, it is telling us that where there is God-ordained structure and authority in our world, if we are walking in the Spirit, we will order ourselves underneath the leadership and direction of the person whom God has placed in authority over us.

Submitting to God-ordained authority in our lives is hard! But—and we'll get to this more later—so is the Spirit-filled exercise of godly leadership. It is active servant leadership. It is sacrificial. Both spouses are called to something joyful, but at the same time, something very challenging.

The biblical idea of headship is never about entitlement or privilege. It's never self-seeking or self-serving. If a husband's leadership is focused on getting his way or serving his preferences, he's not loving his wife. He's abusing his role. At the same time, if a wife is refusing to yield to her husband's godly, loving leadership in her marriage, and is instead seeking to control or manipulate her spouse in order to have things her way, she is not loving her husband as she ought.

Talk Together

1. What are practical ways you seek to love your wife as Christ loves the church? What is an example of how you have sought to submit to your husband as the church submits to Christ? Are there areas you can each grow here?

2. What are healthy ways we can challenge each other to keep ourselves from being self-serving as we face critical decisions and key moments in life?

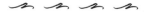

Now, because of sinful abuses of the leadership/submission paradigm for marriage, there are clarifications and disclaimers necessary whenever this subject is introduced.

1. The Bible does not teach that men are more valuable, have more dignity, have more skill, or are more important than women. Nowhere is that taught. Men and women are equally image-bearers of God. Men and women have equal worth, equal dignity, and equal value. This cannot be stressed enough.

2. The Bible does not teach that women are to submit to men. It teaches that wives are to submit to their own husbands. Single women have no obligation before God to follow the leadership of men, unless those men are in some other position of authority over them.

3. There is a difference between submission and obedience. The Bible teaches that children are to obey their parents. But

the Bible does not teach that women are to obey their husbands. They are to submit—to willingly place themselves under their husband's leadership. That's different than obeying.

So what is the difference? What would submitting and not obeying look like?

Submission means that you acknowledge and affirm the God-ordained structure for marriage, and you willingly choose to embrace your position inside that structure. But if, inside that structure, someone in authority directs you to do something that violates God's Word or that violates your conscience, you respectfully decline and you face the consequences.

That's the case if your government requires you to do something that God forbids. You refuse to submit to the governing authorities in that case. You choose to obey God and not people. You may go to jail. If you do, you entrust yourself to God. He is your strength and your shield.

If your employer requires that you do something that God forbids, you obey God and not your employer. And you may get fired. If you do, you entrust yourself to God. He is your strength and your shield.

And wives, if your husband requires you to do something that God forbids or that violates your conscience, you obey God and not your husband.

Let me add quickly here that if one of the consequences a wife faces for refusing to submit to ungodly leadership is abuse from her husband, she should call the police and have her husband held accountable for his actions. More about that in a minute.

4. Submission also doesn't mean that a wife has no voice and that her husband gets to make all the decisions. It does mean that if a husband and wife are facing a particular issue and they come to a place where they don't agree on the decision they are facing, after a season where the husband has sought and paid careful attention to his wife's input, and after there has been a time for both of them to pray, if the impasse still exists, the husband is the one who will be responsible before the Lord for whatever decision is made.

That's what we see in Genesis 3. Eve was tempted to disobey God. Adam, who was there with her during the temptation, remained silent and did not lead his wife. She did not seek Adam's input or counsel.

And when God addressed the issue with them, whom did he hold accountable? Adam.

Think of it this way: husbands and wives should function kind of like corporate officers in a marriage. The husband is the chief executive officer who is ultimately responsible to the board of directors (in this case, the triune God) for the operation of the marriage. But the wife in this illustration is also a corporate officer. She is the chief operating officer. These corporate officers are together responsible for the success of the family corporation. And the wise CEO is always fully engaged with the COO, heeding the wisdom and insight she provides.

Of course, every analogy breaks down somewhere, and this one isn't exempt. But the point is, at the end of the day, the buck stops with the CEO. He bears that weight and that responsibility.

Talk Together

1. Was the biblical model of authority and submission modeled for you in your family of origin? Was the model you saw healthy or unhealthy? Explain your answer.

2. What has most shaped how you think about the issue of authority and submission in marriage? Society? Your family of origin? The Bible? What percentage would you attach to each?

What should a couple do if they regularly disagree on a wide variety of issues? What if you and your spouse are at odds on everything?

Let me talk to husbands first.

My experience has been that most of the time when a wife is having a hard time respecting and supporting her husband's leadership, it's either because he is being passive and abdicating his authority, or because he is being authoritarian and abusing his authority. In either case, he is being self-serving.

Husbands have a duty to make it as easy as possible for their wives to respond positively to their leadership. Here's how a husband does that:

1. He doesn't start by telling his wife, "Here's what I think we should do." He starts by praying and seeking God's direction for his marriage and his family. In leading his wife, the key

question he asks is not, "What do *I* think is the right decision here?" It's, "What do I believe *God* would have us do?"

It's a whole lot easier for a wife to follow her husband if she's convinced that her husband walks with God, seeks God, and wants to obey God. This is a prerequisite for spiritual leadership in your home. When you're facing hard choices and tough decisions, make sure your wife knows that what matters most to you is not doing what you want, or even what she wants, but what God wants.

2. Remember that as a leader in your marriage, you have a job to do. You are to love, nourish, and cherish your wife. Those words come straight out of Ephesians 5. Loving your wife means you are not self-serving. You regularly put her needs ahead of your own. You sacrifice for her. Nourishing your wife means that you make it your priority to see to it that she is flourishing and growing and bearing fruit in every area of her life—physical, intellectual, recreational, social, spiritual, all of it. Nourishing your wife means that you say, "Of course, I'll watch the kids while you go to the women's Bible study or go for the weekend on the women's retreat. I want you to have that time." Cherishing your wife means that you protect her and value her. It means that she knows she is valued and cared for.

The opposite of being self-seeking as a husband is to love and nourish and cherish your wife. When a man does that, he makes it so much easier for his wife to follow his leadership.

3. A godly husband will regularly and intentionally seek his wife's input and wisdom. And he'll listen carefully to it.

Sometimes when God wants to speak to a husband, he speaks through his wife. Our wives have insight and intuition that we as husbands do not have. They have a perspective on things that we don't. I don't know how many times in talking about things with my wife, she has provided me with insight and perspective that I simply lacked.

If, as a husband, you can't quickly come up with examples of how your wife's insights or thoughts have caused you to reconsider a decision or make a different choice, something is wrong in how you're leading.

If your wife knows she's being heard and valued and her ideas are being considered and not dismissed, it's a lot easier for her to respond to your leadership.

4. It's not your job to teach your wife how to submit to you.

I was having a conversation once with a coworker who had been married for about six months. I asked him how his marriage was doing.

"It's going okay," he told me. "But honestly, my wife is having a hard time submitting to my leadership."

I smiled. I asked, "Where in the Bible does it say she should do that?"

He looked at me with surprise and said, "It's in Ephesians 5!"

I said, "Turn there and read the passage to me."

He turned to Ephesians 5:22 and started to read. "Wives, subm—"

"Wait. Stop. What's the first word in that verse again?"

"It's *wives*."

"Are you a wife?"

"No."

"Okay then. You can skip that verse. It's not for you."

My coworker got the point. A wife's choice to submit to her husband is between her and God. It's not a husband's job to teach his wife to submit to him, much less to demand that she do so.

Here's my counsel to a wife who finds that she regularly disagrees with her husband:

- Ask yourself if your heart and attitude are right before the Lord. Are you filled with the Spirit and walking with the Spirit?
- Ask yourself why is it that you so regularly don't agree? Is it possible that some of the fault lies on your end? Are you a disagreeable person? Are you a controlling person? Are you a fearful person? Are you humble and teachable? Do you think that your way is always the right way?
- Do you demonstrate respect for your husband? Does he know that you are his ally and not his enemy?
- Have you sought outside godly counsel about major areas where you disagree (not gossiping or getting friends to support your position)?
- Do you know what it looks like to respectfully appeal?
- Do you pray for your husband?
- Do you trust God?

Russell Moore makes the point that submitting to someone is different than agreeing with that person. If you agree on something, submission isn't necessary. You're not submitting until you're facing an issue where you don't agree.[3] Again, submission means you are choosing to place yourself under another person's leadership when you don't agree on an issue.

There's one more very important caveat for wives here. Some have so misunderstood or misapplied the biblical teaching on submission that they have suggested that a woman in an abusive relationship should continue submitting to her husband.

That is absolutely not the case. Anyone who says otherwise is twisting the Scriptures and putting women in danger.

Pastor and author Justin Holcomb defines an abusive relationship as "a pattern of coercive, controlling, or abusive behavior that is used by one individual to gain power and control over another. It's not just physical—it includes emotional abuse, spiritual abuse."[4] Abuse is all about gaining power and control over another person. Abusing another human being is a deeply rooted, pernicious sin. And it's never an act of love to allow someone to continue in sin.

Any wife who feels threatened by her husband or who is experiencing abuse needs to get help—first for herself and then for her husband. If she believes she is in danger, she needs to call the police. She needs to make sure she's safe. Assuming she's in a church where the church leaders are functioning as they should, she should enlist their help. They have a responsibility to protect her—involving civil authorities when abuse has occurred, as well as addressing her husband's sin and holding him accountable for his actions.

Most of the time when people have a problem with the bibli-cal idea of husbands leading and wives submitting in marriage, what they really have a problem with is one of two things.

1. They've either seen the headship and sub-mission idea lived out by proud, self-serving, ungodly men who think they're supposed to be the king of the castle and everyone is supposed to bow to them.

or

2. They read Ephesians 5 and think, *I've never heard of anything so oppressive in my life. I'm not doing that!*

Ladies, if you read Ephesians 5 and find yourself thinking, *That can't be right. I'm not doing that,* here's what you're saying, "I know better what works for me than God does. We're doing this my way, not God's way."

That's how Bunny Wilson felt the first time she read Ephesians 5. As a young Christian who grew up without a model of a godly marriage, she was taught to be a strong and indepen-dent woman.

She remembers:

> When I came to Christ, Christianity, I came from being an atheist. So when I fell in love, when I finally came to meet Jesus Christ, and I fell in love with Jesus, I fell in love with his Word, and so I started reading it and eating and eating it and eating it. And then one day I

ran across a Scripture that said, "Wives, submit yourselves unto your own husbands as unto the Lord," and my first thought was, *Why would God mess up a good book with a Scripture like that?*[5]

Bunny went on to say that when she finally began to wrestle with the idea of submission, what she began to realize was how her heart and mind had been clouded by anger, manipulation, guile, and stubbornness.

And her husband, Frank, said, "When Bunny decided to become submissive, it put the fear of God in my heart. Because I knew I was no longer contending with her. I was now dealing directly with God."[6]

Bunny said, "I had been standing in the way, and God wanted to get at Frank. He couldn't get to Frank because I was blocking. I was intercepting the whoopin', I was getting the whoopin', when what God wanted was a clear shot at Frank!"[7]

There's a reason why this issue matters so much.

Why does God put a structure in marriage? Why doesn't he just say, "You guys work it out. Do whatever works best for you."

In Ephesians 5, God says that it is his intention that marriage be a picture for the whole world of the relationship between Jesus and his church. In the middle of explaining that husbands are to love their wives sacrificially and not in a self-serving way, and that wives are to respect and submit to their husbands, Paul writes, "This mystery is profound, and I am saying that it refers to Christ and the church" (Eph. 5:32). What is the mystery? Two becoming one in marriage. And why is it profound? Because it points to the gospel. One of the main purposes God has for marriage is to provide a living illustration of Jesus' love for his bride, the church.

Is there mutual submission between Jesus and his church? Does he ever place himself under our authority? Of course not. By God's design, a wife's role in marriage is to be a living picture of how the church of Jesus Christ joyfully submits to his authority and leadership.

On the other hand, is Jesus harsh toward his church? Is he proud and arrogant? Is he ever abusive or manipulative? Of course not. By God's design, a husband's role in marriage is to model and demonstrate how Jesus sacrificially loves and serves his bride, the church.

This isn't just about function. There is a gospel purpose here.

Talk Together

1. Would you say your thinking about the roles of husbands and wives in marriage has been shaped more by culture or by Scripture?

2. Read Ephesians 5:22–33. Husbands, what is God saying to you in this passage about how you can do a better job of loving and serving your wife? And wives, what is God saying to you about how you can do a better job of honoring and respecting your husband?

Now I have to stop here and raise an issue for you.

So far, I have explained how all these characteristics of love found in 1 Corinthians 13 also describe God, right? God is patient, God is kind, God is not envious, God does not boast, God is not arrogant, God is not rude, God does not insist on his own way . . .

Hang on there. Is that right? Doesn't God insist on his own way?

When God commands us to live our lives according to his precepts, is he violating his own definition of love? Is he insisting on his own way?

Here is where we have to understand that the central characteristic of authentic, biblical *agape* love is for a person to put someone else's welfare ahead of self-interest. And so while God does, indeed, insist on his own way, he does so because doing life his way is in our best interest.

Parents understand this. We have children who are naturally bent toward insisting on their own way. When they were babies and they were hungry, if we failed to attend to their needs immediately, they made their demands known regardless of how tired we were or what time it was.

And as they became toddlers, we still saw a deep root of ingrained selfishness in them, right? In fact, we have a term we use for two- or three-year-olds who insist on their own way. This is the age group that is most closely associated with the word *tantrum*. We often call this period of life the "terrible twos."

Part of our assignment as parents is to train and correct this kind of self-seeking behavior in our children. When we insist that they obey us, we are preparing them to respond rightly to God-ordained authority in their lives. It is with their best interest at heart that we teach them to follow our leadership.

God insists on our obedience, just as we do with our children. But it's not because God is self-seeking. He insists on his own way for our sake, because everything in the universe functions the way it should when things are done God's way.

In marriage, we have to confront the reality that our self-seeking, "my way or the highway" approach to life is bone deep in every one of us. There is a reason self-seeking comes naturally.

Before they rebelled against God, Adam and Eve loved him and loved each other and loved the world God had created for them more than they loved themselves. Adam realized before the fall that his greatest joy and happiness in life was found in loving and serving and glorifying God, loving and serving Eve, and caring for the world God had made.

But Adam was not motivated to obey God because of self-interest. Adam loved and served God and his wife because he recognized that the God who created the world and everything in it is worthy and deserving of his full devotion and love.

When Adam rebelled against God, his thinking had become corrupted and twisted. Now, Adam was rejecting God and his ways. Now he was loving himself. He was declaring his independence from God. He wasn't living to serve or please God anymore; he was living only to please himself.

In fact, in his corrupted thinking, Adam now hated God, because he saw God as an impediment to his happiness, not as the source of his happiness. He thought God was holding out on him.

What Adam did at that point is what all of us do when we reject God. He declared himself the sole authority over his own life. He said, "I know best; I'll do it my way."

It is the nature of humanity apart from God to set up self in the place of God and to make an idol of self. Instead of being devoted to God and loving him supremely, a man apart from God is devoted to self and loves self supremely.

But when God redeems us, we start to see our self-love for what it really is. And we are moved to repent—to turn away from self-serving self-love. When we experience the new birth, the spiritual reawakening that comes when we surrender our lives to God, he restores in us a desire that has been dormant ever since Adam's rebellion: a desire to honor and serve him and to care for the needs of others.

We still have old habits and desires that keep us from loving God and others as we should. But when God begins the spiritual renovation project in us that we so desperately need, we begin to see our self-serving approach to love as the ugly sin that it is. As new men and women in Christ, we are given both the capacity and the power to love God and love others in a selfless way, because now we have the source of selfless love living in us and loving through us.

Jesus is both the source and the model for what love looks like when it does not seek its own. Jesus never insisted on his own way, but instead was fully devoted to God and his plan and purposes for his life, and to our good, even at great cost to himself.

In John 4, right after the encounter with the Samaritan woman at the well, Jesus' disciples were urging him to eat something. In verses 32–34, he said to his disciples, "'I have food to eat that you do not know about.' So the disciples said to one another, 'Has anyone brought him something to eat?' Jesus said to them, 'My food is to do the will of him who sent me and to accomplish his work.'"

In other words, Jesus was saying, "Doing all that God has sent me to do is what gives me life. It sustains me and keeps me alive." His greatest joy was found in doing the will of the Father.

Jesus' self-emptying love for us was on display in the Garden of Gethsemane as he prayed the most poignant prayer in all of Scripture: "My Father, if it be possible, let this cup pass from me; nevertheless, not as I will, but as you will" (Matt. 26:39). Even as he walked to the cross, obeying God was more important to Jesus than life itself.

As we become more like Christ, we increasingly shed our self-serving motivations and increasingly value obedience to God.

Jonathan Edwards, in his sermons on 1 Corinthians 13, made the point that when you give up on self-seeking and surrender to Jesus and his plan for your life, you are serving your own interests in a way that a self-serving approach to life can never accomplish. When we insist on our own way, it's because we believe that life will be better for us if we make things go the way we think they should. But Edwards reminds us that we will never know the blessing of God as long as we continue insisting on our own way.

You are not your own. As you have not made yourself, you were not made for yourself. You are neither the author nor the end of your own being. Nor is it you that uphold yourself in being, or that provide for yourself. There is another that hath made you, and preserves you, and provides for you, and on whom you are dependent: And He hath made you for Himself and for the good of your fellow creatures, and not only for yourself. He has placed before you higher and nobler ends than self, even the welfare of your fellowmen, and of society and the interests of His kingdom; and for these you ought to labor and live, not only in time, but for eternity. . . .

Therefore, you must not henceforth treat yourself as your own, by seeking your own interests or pleasure only, or even chiefly; for if you do so, you will be guilty of robbing Christ. And as you are not your own, so nothing that you have is your own. Your abilities of body and mind, your outward possessions, your time, talents, influences, comforts—none of them are your own; nor have you any right to use them as if you had absolute property in them, as you will be likely to do if you imagine them only for your own private benefit, and not for the honor of Christ and for the good of your fellowmen.

If you place your happiness in God, in glorifying Him and in serving Him by doing good—in this way, above all others, you will promote your wealth, and honor, and pleasure here below, and obtain hereafter a crown of unfading glory and pleasures forevermore at God's right hand.

If you seek not your own, but the things of Christ and the good of your fellowmen, God Himself will be yours, and Christ yours, and the Holy Spirit yours, and all things yours.[8]

Talk Together

1. Think about one area in your marriage where you most often insist on your own way. If you are not yet married, think about one area of your life where you most insist on your own way. What is the chief motive behind your insistence? Is it self-serving, or is it about serving others?

2. How can you help one another cultivate a gracious, humble spirit that does not demand its own way?

CHAPTER 6

Keep Calm and Keep Loving: Love Is Unflappable

Love is not rude.
It is not irritable or resentful.
—1 Corinthians 13:5

More than a decade after he died, Fred Rogers was suddenly once again in the cultural spotlight.

In 2018, on what would have been Mr. Rogers' ninetieth birthday, filmmaker Morgan Neville released the trailer for a documentary he had been working on about the children's television star. It was called *Won't You Be My Neighbor?* The film was released in theaters a few months later to critical acclaim and box office success. Audiences made it the highest grossing biographical documentary film of all time.

A year later, actor Tom Hanks played Mr. Rogers in a film called *A Beautiful Day in the Neighborhood.* The children's television icon who has been teased and satirized over the years for his extreme gentleness and kindness was all of a sudden being revered and remembered with great fondness. A generation that had grown up learning from an ordained Presbyterian minister and his puppets about how to process their emotions was suddenly longing to reconnect with their teacher.

At a time when the level of civil and political discourse in the United States was devolving into contempt, anger, cynicism, and sarcasm, people found themselves longing for someone who might remind us all of how we are supposed to treat one another. As it turns out, Mr. Rogers was the perfect candidate. He had spent a lifetime modeling what loving your neighbor looks like.

Fred Rogers, by his own admission, was not a perfect man. But by all accounts, what we saw on TV was not an act. Fred was Fred when the cameras were rolling and when they stopped. And while King Friday may have occasionally been guilty of being rude or irritable, you can search all 912 episodes of *Mister Rogers' Neighborhood* and not find any trace of rudeness or irritability or resentment from the host of the program.

Most of us don't have Fred Rogers' personality or temperament. But the kind of gentle, compassionate, and empathetic love he exhibited toward children is a picture of the kind of love described in 1 Corinthians 13. Your spouse may never put on a cardigan and slippers and adopt Mr. Rogers' persona, and you might not want them to. But that's not the point, is it? Every marriage would benefit from a little more of the kindness for which Fred Rogers was so widely known.

Rudeness, irritability, and resentment are love killers. The way we speak to one another in marriage reflects what's really in our hearts. Jesus said, "Out of the abundance of the heart the mouth speaks" (Matt. 12:34). But rudeness, irritability, and resentment go well beyond the things we say to one another. When those malignancies are resident in our hearts, they metastasize in all kinds of ways. These three menaces travel as a team. And wherever they go, love is never with them.

We would never think to describe someone who is acting rudely as a loving person. The same is true for anyone who is regularly irritable or resentful. Whenever rudeness, irritability, and resentment are present, they run love right out of the room.

If our goal in our relationships—especially in marriage—is to love our neighbor as ourselves (Matt. 22:39), then we have to root out rudeness, irritability, and resentment. We have to replace those stubborn habits with godly character qualities like kindness, compassion, humility, meekness, and patience. A loving marriage will not grow or thrive when spouses are routinely rude to one another. When a spouse is regularly irritable with his or her mate, love is quickly quenched. When resentment lingers, love withers.

The problem is, most people who are rude or irritable or resentful are blind to it. They see it clearly in others, but like the people with logs in their own eyes, they can't see these traits in themselves (Matt. 7:3–5). They may recognize that they are often "annoyed" by things. But they are blind to the way those annoyances provoke them. When they are rude, they believe the object of their disrespect deserved it. When something triggers their irritability, they believe the irritability is justified.

To be committed to love is to be committed to recognizing and putting to death rudeness, irritability, and resentment. And at the same time, husbands and wives must be equally committed to the cultivation of the godly graces that must take root and blossom in their place.

Talk Together

1. Over the next couple of days, take note of what really gets under your skin. At the end of each day, reflect on it, and ask yourself whether you were characterized by a posture of rudeness, irritability, or resentment. Share with your spouse, if you're married.

2. How does it make you feel when you're around someone who is getting annoyed or frustrated all the time? How can you keep from becoming *that* person?

It was sad news for anyone who had come of age during the latter half of the 1900s. On July 3, 2019, *Mad* magazine announced that after almost seventy years of tutoring an audience made up of mostly young males in snark and sarcasm, the magazine had printed its final edition.

I subscribed to *Mad* magazine when I was in my early teens. I read the magazine cover to cover. I was particularly fond of one recurring feature: Al Jaffe's "Snappy Answers to Stupid Questions." Mr. Jaffe made an art form out of what we used to call "the put-down." He would create a cartoon where one person asked a question with an obvious answer. He would then offer his readers a choice of three possible "snappy answers" for the question, along with a space where the reader could provide his own retort.

I remember one cartoon panel that showed a woman sitting in the waiting room of a doctor's office that had four or five No Smoking signs prominently displayed. She pulled out a cigarette and lighter and asked the office manager, "Mind if I smoke?" While I don't remember all three possible responses, the one that has stuck with me since my days in junior high was, "Why? Are you on fire?"

In my home, teasing and humor were expressions of endearment. Our poking at each other was playful and not mean-spirited. We expressed our love for one another by being witty and clever.

But sarcasm and teasing were not a big part of the family of origin of my wife, Mary Ann. And that created an interesting dynamic when we got married. I didn't understand why my new wife wasn't charmed and warmed by my witty responses to her questions. I was not prepared to see tears in response to what I regarded as playful banter.

The apostle Peter tells husbands that we are to live with our wives "in an understanding way" (1 Pet. 3:7). In fact, he says that a failure to do so will affect the way God responds to our prayers. I've had to learn over time that even my well-intentioned words can be misunderstood. I can wound my wife even when what I'm trying to do is express affection. I can be rude even when that's not my intent.

Being rude seems like such a little thing, doesn't it?

Most of us think that the opposite of rudeness is politeness. A rude person is someone who doesn't use good manners. It's someone who doesn't wait until everyone has been served before starting to eat. Or someone who burps after a meal (or in some Asian cultures, someone who doesn't burp).

When the Bible says love is not rude, it is talking about something more than adhering to a set of social graces. The word for rude is a Greek word that can be used for a wide range of behavior, from bad manners to shameful acts. Alexander Strauch offers a long list of actions that might qualify as rudeness: "inappropriate dress, inconsiderate talk, disregard for other people's time or moral conscience, taking advantage of people, tactlessness, ignoring the contributions or ideas of others, running roughshod over others' plans or interest, inappropriate behavior with the opposite sex, basic discourtesy and rudeness, and general disregard for proper social conduct."[1]

These things, Strauch says, are all evidence of a lack of love for others. They have no place in the life of a believer.

Rudeness describes the way we treat others when we think we are better than they are. Phil Ryken says, "Using bad manners may seem like a small failing, if we think it is a failing at all. But the Bible says when we do not treat people nicely and properly, we are failing to love, which is always our calling, even in the little things."[2]

Think about this practically for a second. Someone buys you a gift. You do not write a thank-you note. Here is what you have just said to that person. "Even though you took time, spent money, and went to the effort to buy something nice for me, I am too busy with other things to take five minutes to write you a note. You and your kindness are just not that much of a priority in my life."

Rudeness comes from a heart of arrogance. Rude people are intently focused on how the behavior of others affects them, but they pay virtually no attention to how their behavior affects others, even in little things.

When the Christians in Corinth got together for church and to celebrate the Lord's Supper, rudeness was the order of the day. Paul rebuked them for their behavior in 1 Corinthians 11, just two chapters before this "love chapter":

> When you come together, it is not the Lord's supper that you eat. For in eating, each one goes ahead with his own meal. One goes hungry, another gets drunk. What! Do you not have houses to eat and drink in? Or do you despise the church of God and humiliate those who have nothing? What shall I say to you? Shall I commend you in this? No, I will not. (vv. 20–22)

And then look at verses 33–34:

> So then, my brothers, when you come together to eat, wait for one another—if anyone is hungry, let him eat at home—so that when you come together it will not be for judgment. About the other things I will give directions when I come.

These people were just plain rude. Not thinking of others at all.

Hudson Taylor, the great missionary to China, once explained how important politeness and tact were to his missionary efforts.

He said that his sensitivity to Chinese customs and culture were a vital part of his efforts to make Christ known to those he was trying to reach.

If you, as a representative of Jesus, are rude and unbecoming, how many people do you think will want to hear your message of forgiveness and grace and mercy? Not many.

Contrast rudeness with the attitude the apostle Paul had displayed when he was with the members of the church in Corinth.

> . . . I have made myself a servant to all, that I might win more of them. To the Jews I became as a Jew, in order to win Jews. To those under the law I became as one under the law (though not being myself under the law) that I might win those under the law. To those outside the law I became as one outside the law (not being outside the law of God but under the law of Christ) that I might win those outside the law. To the weak I became weak, that I might win the weak. I have become all things to all people, that by all means I might save some. I do it all for the sake of the gospel, that I may share with them in its blessings. (1 Cor. 9:19–23)

Paul, of course, wasn't the only one to set aside his preferences out of love for others. Jesus modeled a kind of love that was completely absent of arrogance or rudeness on the night before his crucifixion.

> It was just before the Passover Feast. Jesus knew
> that the time had come for him to leave this
> world and go to the Father. Having loved his
> own who were in the world, he now showed
> them the full extent of his love. (John 13:1 NIV)

This verse marks the beginning of John's account of the death and resurrection of Jesus. His death was the act that demonstrated what the Bible calls the full extent of Jesus' love. But hours before he went to the cross, Jesus provided his disciples with a remarkable and, indeed, shocking demonstration of his love for them.

Jesus' disciples had no idea of what the events of the next twenty-four hours would hold as they arrived in the Upper Room to begin the celebration of the Passover with the traditional Passover meal. If anything, the disciples had been wondering if this was the time when Jesus would inaugurate his kingdom and begin to rule as the Messiah.

So to arrive in the Upper Room for the Passover meal with the man you believe is about to be revealed as the long-awaited Messiah and King of Israel who would lead the nation back to glory, and to find him there with a towel hanging from his belt and a basin of water, insisting that he wash your feet—the job that belongs to the lowest of the household servants—would've been utterly shocking for these followers of Jesus. When Jesus took the towel and the basin and began to wash his disciples' feet, he was performing a living parable that showed his generosity, humility, and courtesy. In other words, he showed that his love was not arrogant or rude.

LOVE LIKE YOU MEAN IT

In the midst of this scene, Peter pulled a classic Peter:

> He came to Simon Peter, who said to him,
> "Lord, do you wash my feet?" Jesus answered
> him, "What I am doing you do not understand
> now, but afterward you will understand." Peter
> said to him, "You shall never wash my feet."
> (John 13:6–8a)

Peter's refusal to allow Jesus to wash his feet seems to reflect a heart of humility. "Jesus," Peter says, "you shouldn't be doing this! I won't let you lower yourself to serve me like this!" This led one Bible commentator to note, "Peter was humble enough to recognize the incongruity of having his feet washed by Jesus, but not humble enough to refrain from telling his Master what not to do!"[3]

Put yourself in Jesus' sandals for just a minute here. This is his last night with his disciples. He is hours from being tortured and executed. He is facing the full extent of human grief and stress—the kind of stress that will manifest itself as he sweats drops of blood later that same evening.

How would you have responded to Peter's defiant outburst if it had been you in that moment? How do you typically respond when someone says no to you?

It would not be uncommon for a rude person to become annoyed in a moment like this. A rude person would probably say something like, "Fine. You don't want me to wash your feet? Step aside, Peter. In fact, I've had about enough of you. Why don't you just get your stuff and leave?"

But that's not Jesus. No, Jesus patiently and kindly explains to Peter, "If I do not wash you, you have no share with me" (John 13:8b).

And then, when Peter goes overboard on the other side and says, "Lord, not my feet only but also my hands and my head!" (v. 9), Jesus once again patiently explains that it's just Peter's feet that need to be washed.

The contrast between Jesus' response to Peter and the rude way you or I often respond when someone won't go along with our plan is profound. It should cause us to think carefully about the traces of arrogance or disrespect for others that we harbor in our own hearts and that show up way too often in our marriage.

In a helpful booklet on 1 Corinthians 13 called *How's Your Love Life?*, Bible teacher Nancy DeMoss Wolgemuth offers some valuable diagnostic questions for us to consider as we think about the extent to which arrogance is a part of our lives:

- Do you have an accurate assessment of your strengths and weaknesses?
- Do you harbor a spirit of pride—an inflated view of yourself?
- Do you feel your spiritual gift is superior to others' gifts?
- Do you communicate an attitude of spiritual superiority toward your husband? Your family? Your work associates?[4]

And what about rudeness?

- Do you have good manners?

- Are you courteous to others, especially in your home?
- Are you tactful—sensitive to the feelings of others and choosing words carefully—so you don't needlessly offend?
- Are you agreeable when you must disagree with someone?
- Do you use sarcasm or put-downs that show disrespect?[5]

You can undoubtedly think of people you know who are ruder than you. But when we compare ourselves to Jesus, we all come up way short, don't we?

Talk Together

1. Can you think of a time recently when you may have been rude to someone, either intentionally or unintentionally? What should you have done in that moment?

2. Look back at the questions from Nancy DeMoss Wolgemuth. Share with your spouse which question helped to expose a hidden trace of arrogance or rudeness in you.

Irritability is a close relative of rudeness. Rude actions or words often spring from the heart of someone who is easily irritated.

When I was growing up, I remember hearing my mom refer to some people as "touchy." She didn't mean that these people liked to hug or put their hands on you. She had in mind people who are hypersensitive or easily provoked to anger. We sometimes talk about having to walk on eggshells around certain people. I have a friend who grew up in a home where her father went to bed each night at nine o'clock. He wanted the house quiet so his sleep would not be disturbed. That was no easy task when there were five children under age ten at home. Any noise would make him irritable, and when he became irritated, the whole house was on edge.

We've already seen that love is patient, that it "suffers long." Being easily irritated is the antithesis of patience.

Our children love to recount what happened during a family road trip when they were still young. I was scheduled to speak at a FamilyLife Weekend to Remember Marriage Getaway in Orlando that coincided with the beginning of our children's spring break. So we decided I would fly to Orlando on Thursday, speak at the conference, and Mary Ann and the kids would leave on Saturday for the two-day drive to central Florida, where they would join me. The plan was that they would drive 600 miles the first day from Little Rock, Arkansas, to Macon, Georgia, so the second day's drive would be a shorter distance—about 350 miles.

Mary Ann was the only licensed driver on the trip. She had been behind the wheel for about eleven hours when they hit the outskirts of Atlanta, an hour away from Macon and a good night's sleep. That's when they found themselves on the interstate-turned-parking lot that was I-285 on the west side of

Atlanta. It wasn't stop-and-go traffic; it was stop, no-go traffic. It took them an hour to travel three miles.

The family finally arrived in Macon an hour later than planned. Mary Ann was trying to find both a place where everyone could eat dinner and the location of the hotel. Being in an unfamiliar location, she wound up making a sharper than expected turn. As she did, our youngest son, David, yelled from the back of the van, "I just spilled all my jelly beans!" Sure enough, the floor of the mini van was now covered with David's jelly beans. His siblings had compassion, but not his mom. She announced to everyone, "There's no sympathy left!"

The kids didn't quite know what to make of Mary Ann's cry of exasperation. But for the rest of the trip, and all the way down to today, the phrase "there's no sympathy left" gets used in our family with a grin anytime things get a little stressful.

We've all had our "no sympathy left" moments. We've all been depleted and exhausted, with no more margin. We've all been irritated. And when we're irritated, it's not just sympathy that vanishes. When irritability takes over, there's no love left. Love has left the building.

Think for a minute about the last time you were irritated by something your spouse said or did. Or maybe it was something your spouse didn't say or didn't do that left you peeved.

Recently, I was home alone for a few days while Mary Ann was traveling to visit family. In our neighborhood, trash is collected on Mondays, while items set aside for recycling are picked up curbside on the same day but only twice a month. It was Sunday afternoon and I had just finished taking both our trash and our recycling to the curb to be picked up the following day when I received a text from my wife reminding me that this was a recycling week and I should make sure our recycle bin was in place.

Guess what my first impulse was upon receiving that helpful text from my wife . . . I was annoyed. Here are some of the thoughts that flashed across my mind in the millisecond after I read the text:

> *Does she think I'm unable to take care of myself?*
> *Does she think I'm incompetent?*
> *I don't need a mother, thank you!*

That's a brief summary of what I was thinking. You get the tone, right?

I was irritated because, without thinking, I ascribed a motive to Mary Ann's text. But it didn't take long before the Spirit of God began to gently nudge me. Here were some of my next thoughts.

> *She wasn't assigning you a chore.*
> *She knows you have a lot going on right now.*
> *She was trying to be helpful.*

The human impulse to be irritated by the words or actions of others is not an impulse born of love and grace. It's not a Spirit-inspired impulse. It comes from the darker part of who we are. Irritation happens when we're focused on ourselves. It's appears when we find ourselves being inconvenienced or disrespected or disregarded or ignored. We end up responding in a way that demonstrates our displeasure with how we think we're being treated.

Jesus was never irritable, although he had plenty of opportunities to be. We might find ourselves reading irritability and impatience into what Jesus said when he rebuked the disciples for their lack of faith. When a man came to Jesus asking for his son to be healed from seizures, saying, "I brought him to your disciples, and they could not heal him" (Matt. 17:16), Jesus responded with what sounds like irritation to us. He says, "O faithless and twisted generation, how long am I to be with you? How long am I to bear with you? Bring him here to me" (v. 17).

But Jesus' words of rebuke and lament in that moment weren't rooted in irritation. They were words of instruction and correction, bringing the disciples face-to-face with what was lacking in them.

We can correct someone else's actions without being short-tempered. This is where the wisdom of Ephesians 4:15 comes into play. There, we're told to speak the truth to others in love. When something our spouse does provokes us, we don't ignore our frustration or fail to reprove or correct one another. But love requires that we drain any lingering irritability out of our correction. Our motive for speaking the truth to each other must always be a desire to see the life of Jesus being fully lived out in one another. We speak the truth to help one another grow in Christlikeness, not because something they've done has left us personally annoyed or offended.

Writing to his protégé Timothy, the apostle Paul coached the young pastor in what is required of one who is called to serve the Lord in pastoral ministry. "Pursue righteousness, faith, love, and peace," he wrote. "The Lord's servant must not be quarrelsome but kind to everyone, able to teach, patiently enduring evil, correcting his opponents with gentleness" (2 Tim. 2:22, 24–25a).

That same wise counsel applies to married couples. How would our marriages be different if, instead of being easily annoyed or irritated with one another, we made it our goal to pursue righteousness, faith, love, and peace? How would our marriages be different if we were not quarrelsome? If we were kind, patient, and gentle as we interacted with each other? If we made sure that any time we spoke the truth, the person hearing us was able to hear our love for them as loudly as they could hear our truth-telling?

If you are an easily provoked, easily irritated person (and if you're not sure, just ask your spouse!), realize that the source of your irritability is not the actions of others. It's your flesh-based response to those actions. People don't make you irritable; a lack of love for God and for others is what makes you irritable. A failure to walk in the power of the Holy Spirit is what makes you irritable.

Talk Together

1. Do you think those closest to you would call you an irritable person?

2. How does dwelling on the gospel help to rid you of irritability?

What about resentment? Follow me here.

There is a link between justice and resentment.

One of God's attributes is that he is just. He is fair. He will not allow wickedness to go unpunished.

At the same time, God is loving. He is merciful and gracious. And just as his love, mercy, and grace don't diminish his justice, so his justice does not diminish other aspects of his divine character.

He is perfectly loving and perfectly just. It's possible to be both.

But we are fallen men and women. When it comes to being loving and just, we can easily drift to a place where love becomes conditional and where what we think is justice is really resentment.

In their book *Forgiveness Therapy*, psychologists Robert Enright and Richard Fitzgibbons say resentment is:

> an unhealthy response to injustice, sometimes an injustice that won't quit—such as continual demeaning comments from a partner, or the unreasonable demands of a boss who just doesn't "get it." Resentment in cases like these represents a development in one's anger from mild to deeper—and it lingers. This kind of resentment can lead to unhappiness, continual irritability, and psychological compromise, including excessive anxiety and depression.[6]

The words that are translated as "resentful" in the English Standard Version of the Bible are actually three Greek words that literally mean "to count up wrongdoing." The New International Version says that resentment involves keeping a "record of wrongs." Eugene Peterson, in The Message paraphrase of the Bible, says love makes no room for resentment. It "puts up with anything."

You cannot be loving and harbor resentment at the same time. Keeping a record of wrongs will extinguish love as it pushes you away from another person. At the same time, holding onto an attitude of resentment doesn't make you particularly lovable. Resentment is not an attractive feature.

In a word, resentment is poison to a relationship. It will destroy your marriage. And it will destroy you in the process.

Our perfectly just Creator has implanted in every human heart a desire for justice and fairness. Sin shifts the issue from justice as God defines it to justice as we define it. Once that shift is made, we become hyper-focused on ways in which others have treated us unfairly. And that's where resentment is born.

For years, couples have heard people extol the benefits of a "50-50 marriage." The idea behind the 50-50 approach is that love will flourish in a setting where there is an equal distribution of marital responsibilities and family duties.

It's true that envy and bitterness can easily appear in an out-of-balance marriage, where one partner is passive about the household management or cultivating a healthy relationship. When a spouse isn't doing his or her fair share at home, resentment finds fertile soil in which to grow. But there are so many reasons why the 50-50 approach to marriage doesn't work. The primary reason is because we are all prone to inflate the value of our own contributions to the relationship while minimizing or overlooking the contributions of a spouse. Someone has said that a person who says, "I'll meet you halfway" is often a poor judge of distance.

A 50-50 mind-set introduces performance and evaluation into a relationship that is designed by God to be founded on commitment and self-sacrifice. In a 50-50 marriage, love is withheld when we don't believe our spouse has earned it. And when love is suppressed, couples enter into a downward spiral that leads to isolation and rejection in marriage.

A 50-50 marriage is a works-based marriage; God calls us to a grace-based, gospel-reflecting marriage.

God's love for us is never conditional. It is not performance based. God doesn't withhold love as punishment for our mistakes or transgressions. There is no resentment in God, even when we ignore him.

The father of the prodigal son never stopped loving his boy. When his son came home, the father ran out to meet him. There was not an ounce of resentment or bitterness for the hurt or heartache the wayward son had caused.

My mom told me once that when she and my dad were first married, he told her that she should not expect much help from him during the workweek. He said he needed to maintain his focus on his job from Monday morning until Friday night. Caring for the house and the kids were her job during that time. He'd be available for help around the house or with the kids only on the weekends.

I saw that lived out at home. Dad was usually home for dinner. But once the meal was over, he disappeared into his home office in our basement where he remained until bedtime.

Mom and Dad both grew up during the Depression, and I'm sure part of what motivated my dad to stay focused on his work was a desire to make sure he provided for us. In that era, this approach to the division of labor between husbands and wives was fairly common. I imagine my mom resigned herself to the arrangement without much protest.

But that doesn't mean that she was immune to the resentment that can begin to build up in a marriage when one partner is having lunch with coworkers each day while the other partner is fixing mac and cheese for kids who still aren't potty-trained. When a husband or a wife starts to feel like he or she is bearing more weight than the other, the pollen of resentment is in the air.

The problem with resentment is what it leads to. The fruit of resentment is bitterness. Resentment stirs in us a desire for revenge, to even the score and return evil for evil. But the Bible is clear that children of God are to let go of resentment and leave justice to God, who alone is able to judge matters with perfect justice and fairness (Rom. 12:17–19). Do not return evil for evil, Peter wrote, but give a blessing instead (1 Pet. 3:9). Paul, in a Roman prison, wrote to Timothy telling him that a mutual acquaintance of theirs, Alexander the coppersmith, had done Paul great harm. But as quickly as he acknowledged the injury suffered, Paul released it. "The Lord will repay him according to his deeds" (2 Tim. 4:14). Case closed. Resentment released.

That's the counsel of Scripture for us when we feel we are being ignored or disregarded by our mate, or when it seems we are carrying the heaviest part of the load in our marriage. The Bible tells us to entrust ourselves to God.

My dad died when he was sixty-eight. It wasn't long after his death that my mom moved from the home they had lived in to a retirement community. She told me one day that she could usually tell whether the other people she met in the retirement community were widowed or divorced. "I can see it in their faces," she said. "There is a hardness or a tightness there in the faces of so many of the people I've met who have been through a divorce. But with the widows and widowers, even in their loss, I can see peace."

What I think my mom was seeing in the faces of so many who had been through a divorce was a lack of peace fueled by a lingering resentment for having been mistreated or abandoned by a spouse.

Talk Together

1. Can you think of times when you have found yourself counting up the ways your spouse has displeased you in some way? Instead of allowing resentment to build, what's a healthy way to address your frustrations?

2. In what ways would you say the 50-50 mind-set affects how you think about your relationship? How does that thinking tend to affect your marriage?

KEEP CALM AND KEEP LOVING: LOVE IS UNFLAPPABLE

Rudeness, irritability, and resentment will drain the life and love out of any marriage. So is there an antidote?

There is. The Bible actually prescribes the same antidote for every kind of poisonous behavior that qualifies as a "work of the flesh" (Gal. 5:19ff).

Step one is to identify it. Now, you might need help with this one. If you are blind to your own rudeness or irritability or resentment, have your spouse or other friends help you pinpoint the words or actions that expose your flesh and have become ingrained in how you act. Receive your spouse's input with humility. (That word just keeps showing up, doesn't it?)

Step two is to confess your rude, irritable, or resentful thoughts, words, or actions as sin. These things are not just "rough edges." They're not neutral personality traits. And they're not simply an offense against another person. We have to see these things for what they really are—a declaration to God that our priorities or preferences are supremely important, more important than the feelings or needs of others, and more important than our desire to honor God.

Surfing my way through an online forum, I came across an interesting entry from someone who had become concerned about a pattern of rudeness in his life. Here's what he wrote:

> I become rude when I'm in a bad mood or I'm with someone I don't like. I frown, I speak in short sentences, I see everything negatively, and when someone asks me to do something, I do it hesitantly and without enthusiasm. I do my best to smile and be nice but I often fail, because

the bad mood makes it very painful. I just then
wish my mood would get better somehow. Is it
sin to be rude, and does being rude to people
you don't like count as revenge?[7]

Is it a sin to be rude? Others who posted in answering this
man's question sought to minimize his rudeness. "I doubt any of
those things are a sin," one person wrote. "Having a rude disposi-
tion may not be sinful in itself," said another.

If your goal is to become less rude—or less irritable or
resentful—trying to minimize these characteristics won't help.
And wondering how close you can get to "sin" without actually
sinning is never the place to start. We need to see these traits as
God sees them. If loving your neighbor is one of the two great
commandments, and if love is not rude or irritable or resentful,
then we ought not try to downplay the sinfulness of these traits.
We're not being the people God has created us to be when we are
being rude or irritable or resentful.

Step three begins a process that will enable you to root out
these traits in your life. Think about times in your marriage
when have been provoked and have responded rudely or irritably
or resentfully. What are the circumstances that bring out the
worst in you? One strategy for dealing with any habitual sin
pattern is to avoid as best we can the circumstances that trigger
it. And when those circumstances can't be avoided, we need to
make sure we have our spiritual armor on (Eph. 6:10–20). We
have to prepare ourselves spiritually as we enter into an environment where in the past we have been provoked to sin. We have
to head into those situations dependent on the grace of God

and walking in the power of the Holy Spirit to help us curb our offensive tongues or our ill-mannered behavior. Pray. Ask God to help you. Desire to honor him above all else.

The fourth step is key. When we seek to put to death a particular sinful pattern in our lives, we have to be equally committed to cultivating new ways of speaking or acting toward others. It's not enough to curb our tongues. We have to retrain our tongues. We have to replace rudeness and irritability and resentment with more grace-filled ways of relating to others. Look at the listing of the fruit of the Spirit found in Galatians 5:22–23. Love. Joy. Peace. Patience. Kindness. Goodness. Faithfulness. Gentleness. Self-control. Which of these graces would help root out rudeness and resentment and irritability in your life?

The point is, rooting out sinful patterns happens as we daily learn to walk in the Spirit and to replace our carnal habits with new Spirit-empowered actions and attitudes that reflect God's character. Only God can give us the grace we need to replace our rude, irritable, resentful, self-centered focus with a heart that is kind, gentle, and patient toward others.

Talk Together

1. Do you need to change the way you view rudeness? Explain the ways in which being rude to another person is a sin against God.

2. What is one thing you can do this week to intentionally, purposely live out the fruit of the Spirit as a way to start replacing rudeness with kindness and grace?

CHAPTER 7

It's Never Right to Do What's Wrong: Love Is Virtuous

Love does not rejoice at wrongdoing.
(1 Cor. 13:6a)

*T*here is a clear connection between loving someone and pursuing righteousness. We can't love someone well if we're not simultaneously committed to pursuing godliness. Wrongdoing and love are like oil and water. They don't mix.

You may have noticed: people don't always agree on where the line between right and wrong, moral and immoral, good and evil lies. Even Christians don't always agree. We may have a shared faith and shared common values, but still find ourselves in different places when it comes to applying the Scriptures and living out what we believe. We can find ourselves navigating the gray areas of life very differently.

Here's an example. Say there is this highly-touted, much-talked-about series on HBO. It's one of those series that dominates the discussion at work on the Monday after each new episode is released. People *love* the show.

So you decide to check it out. Online at first. It comes with the TV-MA rating. And HBO lets you know ahead of time what's coming. Adult language. Adult situations. Graphic violence. Brief nudity. Strong sexual content.

Should you check it out?

These kinds of choices can bring tension to a relationship, especially when couples disagree. Not long ago, a friend—a young woman in a dating relationship—pulled me aside to ask my opinion on a conflict she and her boyfriend were having. He wanted her to watch movies that he saw nothing wrong with but that made her uncomfortable. She said that he thought she needed to relax and grow up and engage with themes that reflect what's happening in the real world. She wanted to know if I thought she was being too uptight.

How would you answer her? For that matter, how do you handle the differences between the two of you when it comes to where to draw the line on what you watch and what you don't? I've had Christian couples ask about viewing pornography together as a way to enhance their marital intimacy. If both husband and wife think it's okay, does that mean it is?

Media consumption and entertainment choices are certainly not the only areas where couples might disagree about what's right and wrong. We regularly have to grapple with "wisdom issues"—decisions we face on moral or ethical questions where the Bible does not provide specific instruction.

For Christians, living rightly and making godly choices as we follow Jesus is not a minor issue. "No one born of God makes a practice of sinning," the apostle John tells us, "for God's seed abides in him; and he cannot keep on sinning, because he has been born of God. By this it is evident who are the children of God, and who are the children of the devil: whoever does not practice righteousness is not of God" (1 John 3:9–10). Practicing righteousness clearly matters to God.

So what should you do if you see what looks to you like unrighteousness in your spouse?

When we're dealing with areas where the Bible is clear, we too, must be clear. Where unrighteousness is easy to identify, husbands and wives who have committed themselves to following Jesus and submitting to his authority over their lives should work together to spur one another on to love and good deeds (Heb. 10:24).

Married couples should be allies in the war on sin in each of our lives. Take any of the passages that catalogue for us the "works of the flesh" (start with passages like Galatians 5:19ff or Colossians 3:5ff) and, as a couple, work together on strategies that can help you "put off" or "put to death" the things listed there, from envy and anger to drunkenness and sensuality.

Love does not rejoice at wrongdoing. We don't rejoice in it when we're the one involved, and we don't rejoice when we see it in someone else. It's hard to live with and love someone who stubbornly and habitually makes a practice of rejecting godliness in a particular area of his or her life. But we're not loving our spouse if we're supporting or affirming their sinful patterns or practices. It's not loving to ignore or enable sin. That anemic view of love is often simply disguising a fear of loving confrontation. A failure to speak the truth in love (Eph. 4:15) isn't loving or truthful; it's usually cowardice.

At the same time, we have to be careful we don't drift into the sin of self-righteousness. We are hardwired to become Pharisees, adding our own rules to what God requires and thinking ourselves to be extra spiritual or "super Christians." We easily see specks in our spouse's eyes while we miss the logs in our own.

For example, let's say a husband has a regular routine of taking the first thirty minutes of his day praying and spending time reading and meditating on God's Word. He has found this daily discipline to be not only life-giving, but essential. On those days when circumstances keep him from this regular practice, he can tell a difference in how he thinks and speaks and acts throughout the day. It's hard for him to imagine that anyone who really loves Jesus wouldn't begin their day in the same manner.

Meanwhile, his wife follows a completely different regimen. She sleeps as late as she possibly can and hits the ground running as soon as her alarm goes off. She checks her email and her Facebook feed first thing. She tried for a while setting her alarm to wake up thirty minutes earlier for a quiet time with God. But it didn't work for her.

Over time, it becomes easy for the husband to see his wife's lack of a regular morning routine as a spiritual flaw and a sign of apathy. He starts to see it as "wrongdoing." A sin of omission. And he just wishes she was more godly. Like he is.

Meanwhile, his wife is aware of what her husband is thinking. She's not neglecting time with the Lord, she says. It's just different for her. It's more moment by moment. She prays throughout her day. Isn't that what "pray without ceasing" means? And a lot of her Facebook friends post Bible verses or link to articles and devotionals that she often clicks. Why is her husband so judgmental anyway? She wonders how much good his daily quiet time is actually doing!

As you read that example, I'm guessing you found yourself on one side of the divide or the other. You may have even had a few Bible verses (like the "pray without ceasing" verse) that you were able to pull in to support your position. Or maybe you pull out Psalm 5:3 when David says "O LORD, in the *morning* do I direct my prayers to you!" (emphasis added).

Is either the husband or wife in this illustration guilty of the kind of unrighteousness that a loving spouse should oppose? Love does not endorse or support unrighteousness. But what rises to the level of unrighteousness? What exactly does it mean for us to love one another in marriage by not rejoicing when we see what we believe is "wrongdoing" in our spouse? And what happens to our love for one another when we find ourselves in the moral and spiritual gray areas?

Just what constitutes the wrongdoing that the Bible tells us not to support or rejoice in?

A while back, the word *righteous* found its way again into our cultural lexicon after a long season on the bench. Not long after a school secretary in the 1980s movie *Ferris Bueller's Day Off* reported that the title character was considered by his classmates as a "righteous dude," the word was being employed more regularly, applied to everything from police arrests to certain strains of cannabis. All of a sudden "righteous" was being applied to things with no inherent ethical capabilities, instead of to human behavior.

In the Bible, righteousness means living rightly—living in sync with the way we were designed and how we were created to live. God is the ultimate judge of what is righteous and what isn't. We are living righteous lives when our thoughts and words and actions are in alignment with how God tells us we are to live.

Talk Together

1. Can you think of one or two "wisdom issues" where you've found yourself thinking your spouse was either being too restrictive or too free? Share your thinking with each other and be open to how God might be speaking to you through your spouse.

2. Can you identify an area of spiritual struggle or spiritual weakness in your own life? What is one thing your spouse could do that would help you grow in grace and godliness in that area?

We often fail to see the connection between righteousness and love, but it's clearly there.

All of the commandments of God, Jesus says, can be summed up in two general categories: loving God and loving others. You can't love God and other people and at the same time rejoice in wrongdoing. It's impossible. That's why translators use words like *evil* and *iniquity* as synonyms for unrighteousness or wrongdoing.

The first instance of wrongdoing in human history initiated the unraveling of the love between Adam and Eve, the two that God had made one. Their rebellion against God's command not to eat from the tree in the center of the garden, the tree of the knowledge of good and evil, was a rejection of God's good plan for them and a conscious choice to buy the lie Satan was selling. "You can be like God," he promised. "You can decide for yourself what is right and what is wrong!" (Gen. 3:5, author paraphrase).

That act of wrongdoing on their part had an impact on their marriage. In Genesis 3, when God confronts Adam about their sin, his first response is to blame his wife: "It's the woman's fault!" he said. And he blamed God: "The Woman you gave me" (v. 12 MSG). As soon as they rejected God's plan for them, Adam and Eve started their drift from oneness and love for each other to isolation and blame.

Wrongdoing is the fruit born in a self-centered, self-focused heart. The reason love cannot rejoice at wrongdoing is because our wrongdoing comes from our desire to follow our own path and do our own thing. And focusing on self is the opposite of love.

The people to whom Paul wrote as he lay out his definition of love were notorious for being carnal and flesh-driven instead of being spiritual and Spirit-driven. The church at Corinth was marked by division and disputing, to the point that people were taking one another to civil court. Sexual immorality was rampant. Their practice of the Lord's Supper had become a mockery. And through it all, they were commending themselves for their spirituality. They were a mess, and they had no clue.

Paul says, "Love does not rejoice or get excited when people are living out of sync with the plan of God for their lives" (1 Cor. 13:6, author paraphrase). And to the extent that our lives, our marriages, or our family are not in sync with God's plan for us, our relationships will lack love.

So if we are not to rejoice at unrighteousness, what should we be doing?

And maybe the bigger question is this: How should we respond to our spouse when we believe he or she is out of sync with God's plan? What do we do when we see unrighteousness or "wrongdoing" in them? It's not loving to join in or to celebrate their unrighteousness. And it's not loving to ignore it either. So how should we respond?

We should respond as Jesus responded.

As we read through the Gospels, we should be struck by how Jesus responded when he came face-to-face with people who were living sinful lives.

It was never a "one size fits all" approach with Jesus. When he encountered self-righteous people, he did not hesitate to speak directly with them about their pride and arrogance. He didn't pull any punches. In Matthew 23, for example, he called the scribes and Pharisees a "brood of vipers" and "whitewashed tombs" and "hypocrites."

But more often when he encountered self-righteousness, Jesus' rebuke was measured, as it was with the Rich Young Ruler.

Here was a man who thought he was righteous because of his own law-keeping. Jesus gently exposed the issues that were still present in that young man's life.

Jesus was also gentle with the Pharisees in John 8 who brought to him the woman caught in adultery. He didn't blast them. Instead, he simply and calmly showed them their own sin (v. 7).

So with the self-righteous, Jesus was sometimes gentle and sometimes forceful as he exposed the reality of remaining sin that they either couldn't see or else minimized or dismissed altogether. But there was another group—a group I'll call the "humble unrighteous." With these men and women, Jesus was always gentle. He always demonstrated an overpowering love.

Let me give you some examples:

- The woman caught in adultry in John 8. Jesus loved her and told her to go and sin no more.
- The unrighteous woman in Luke 7 who is identified as "a woman of the city." She was a sinner who interrupted a dinner party Jesus was attending and came and wept and kissed his feet and anointed them with perfume. Jesus said to her, "Your sins are forgiven. . . . Your faith has saved you; go in peace" (vv. 48, 50).
- Matthew, the unrighteous rich tax collector. Jesus called him to become a disciple, and then went to a party at his house with all his unrighteous friends (Matt. 9:9–10).
- Zacchaeus, the unrighteous rich tax collector who wanted to get a look at Jesus but

hid in a tree because he knew he wasn't
worthy. Jesus called him down from the
tree and said, "I must stay at your house
today" (Luke 19:5).

What ought to catch our attention as we read these accounts
from the life of Jesus is how gracious, how kind, how patient, and
how gentle he was in the face of wrongdoing.

Yes, he overturned the moneychangers' tables in the temple.
Yes, he told the Pharisees that they were of their father, the devil.
But more often in the face of ungodliness, Jesus was gentle. He
confronted the sin he saw in the lives of the people around him
with tender concern and kindness.

When there are patterns of wrongdoing or unrighteousness
that we can see in our spouse's life, our job is to be like Jesus—to
follow his example and to humbly, kindly, gently point out their
sin and point them back to him.

The Bible gives us a road map to follow when we see our
spouse in an ongoing pattern of unrighteousness. "If anyone
is caught in any transgression," Paul says in Galatians 6:1–2,
"you who are spiritual should restore him in a spirit of gentleness. Keep watch on yourself, lest you too be tempted. Bear one
another's burdens, and so fulfill the law of Christ."

Is your spouse caught in a pattern of ongoing wrongdoing in
your marriage? Here's what you do:

1. Do some self-examination first. When Paul
   says "you who are spiritual," he's not saying we need to be perfect before we help
   someone else. He's saying we need to ask

ourselves if there is any unrighteousness in our own life that needs to be addressed. Before you try to help your spouse with his or her sins, make sure you address your own sins. Pray the prayer found in Psalm 139:23–24 and ask God to search you and reveal any wrongdoing in your heart. Deal with your own logs before you attempt to help your spouse with his or her specks (Matt. 7:3–5).

2. Make restoration your goal. "You who are spiritual, restore him." The reason for confronting wrongdoing in another person is to see that person restored to righteousness. It's not to shame your husband or your wife. It's not to vent your own anger about their actions or behavior. It's to see your spouse walking rightly with God.

3. Maintain the kind of gentle spirit Jesus modeled when he addressed sin in people's lives. A meek spirit is a spirit that keeps its power in check. There is self-control at work. Kindness toward the transgressor is paramount. If you can't be gentle as you seek to restore a spouse who is trapped in a sinful pattern in his or her life, you're not ready to confront that person.

4. Expect pushback. To confront wrongdoing in someone else is to enter into spiritual

warfare. You are stepping into enemy ter-
ritory. Your goal is to rescue a prisoner of
war from their prison cell. Expect spiritual
opposition. There can be casualties here.
Do not engage in this activity lightly. And
by all means, stay alert. "Keep watch on
yourself."

5. Expect to face temptation yourself as you
engage in this kind of spiritual rescue
operation. It may be temptation to the same
kind of sin. Or it may be a completely different kind of temptation—including the
temptation to pride and self-righteousness,
seeing yourself as better or nobler or more
virtuous than the person you're seeking to
rescue.

Love does not rejoice at unrighteousness. Love does not
celebrate unrighteousness. Love does not endorse, approve of,
ignore, or simply wave away unrighteousness.

At the same time, when love confronts a person who is living
in unrighteousness, love is kind, merciful, and generous in caring
for that person. Love doesn't think, *I'd better make sure they know
I don't approve of their unrighteousness first thing!* Love carefully
and faithfully brings people to Jesus, allowing him to expose the
unrighteousness and address the wrongdoing.

Think back to when God saved you. Think back to how
Jesus came to you and embraced you and loved you. He didn't
say, "You need to clean up your act before I will ever have anything to do with you." Think about how he said to you, "I love

you enough that I died for you. I want you to be with me in my family. I know you have sinned. You are forgiven. I'm here with you. Walk with me, and I'll get your life back in sync."

When Isaiah prophesied about the ministry of the Messiah, he described how the Messiah would address unrighteousness in our lives: "A bruised reed he will not break, and a faintly burning wick he will not quench; he will faithfully bring forth justice" (Isa. 42:3).

Love does not rejoice in wrongdoing. Love confronts it. Wisely. Gently. Carefully. Graciously. Humbly.

Talk Together

1. When was a time someone confronted your wrongdoing in a helpful way? In an unhelpful way?

2. How do you think confronting your own wrongdoing first will help you in confronting the wrongdoing of your spouse?

Mary Ann and I had been married for a number of years when she came to me with an issue for us to think about as a family. We were regular churchgoers. But once church was over, Sunday quickly became like any other day. Mary Ann had begun to wonder if we shouldn't be doing more to "honor the Sabbath day."

We talked about it and made the countercultural decision to take a few activities off the table on Sundays. We kept the TV and our computers off. And we imposed our own blue laws—no shopping on Sundays unless there was an emergency.

All was going fine until September. That's when the NFL started up again. And suddenly, we weren't so single-minded on what our Sundays should look like. Did watching a football game qualify now as "wrongdoing"?

What about the gray areas?

Bible teacher R. C. Sproul wrote, "Each one of us has a system in our heads of what is allowable and what is not allowable in the Christian life. We have a moral code by which we live. Now I doubt if any one of us has a moral system built into our heads that corresponds exactly and precisely in every detail to the moral code that God desires for us. We tend to overlook certain specific things that God commands or forbids, and we also bring baggage into our moral codes where God has left us free. We have this problem then of Christians who are living side by side, but who are not operating with exactly the same moral code."[1]

When wrongdoing is obvious—where there is sexual sin or drunkenness or physical violence or dishonesty—there is no question that a spouse needs to be confronted and the pattern of sin needs to be addressed.

But what do we do when the issues aren't clear-cut?

Remember my friend who was dating that guy who was encouraging her to watch movies with which she was uncomfortable? What if a wife with a tender conscience is married to a husband who loves action films and says, regarding the profanity,

"That's just the way guys in the military talk." Is one person right and the other one wrong?

What about issues that go beyond which movies we watch? What if we're talking about the standards we set for the kids? Or about having a glass of wine or a beer with dinner? Or whether the neighborhood pool, where the standard for modesty is in question, is an okay place to spend a Saturday afternoon? Or how we determine what words meet the biblical standard for wholesomeness?

In Romans 14, the Bible speaks to these kinds of issues. The apostle Paul says that believers are not to quarrel over or pass judgment on others when we're dealing with matters of opinion. While Paul's context in Romans 14 is the local church, that kind of quarreling over matters of opinion can easily become part of our marital dialogue.

Eugene Peterson paraphrases Romans 14:1–2 this way: "Welcome with open arms fellow believers who don't see things the way you do. And don't jump all over them every time they do or say something you don't agree with—even when it seems that they are strong on opinions but weak in the faith department. Remember, they have their own history to deal with. Treat them gently."

As difficult as that can be in a local church setting, the issues are significantly more personal and harder to deal with in marriage.

There were three cultural disputes that were dividing the church at Rome at the time this letter was written: whether it was right to avoid certain kinds of food, whether or not believers should avoid alcohol altogether, and disagreements about matters regarding corporate worship. The Christians in Rome were wrestling with whether these things were matters of personal preference or something more. They needed instruction on what to do when there are matters of personal conscience related to things God has not clearly forbidden or expressly commanded.

The same kinds of issues can lead to division in a marriage. So how do we preserve unity in marriage when we disagree about these wisdom issues?

Right before the apostle Paul offered instruction on dealing with gray areas, he was clear with his readers about the priority of righteousness. He told them they were to "walk properly as in the daytime, not in orgies and drunkenness, not in sexual immorality and sensuality, not in quarreling and jealousy. But put on the Lord Jesus Christ, and make no provision for the flesh, to gratify its desires" (Rom. 13:13–14). There should be no disputing among followers of Jesus about things that are obviously sinful. If someone says, "I think it's okay to quarrel or to be immoral or to be drunk or to be jealous of others," we can respond, "No, those are matters that are beyond dispute in Scripture. God has spoken. That's not how we are to live."

But when it comes to the gray areas, Romans 14 says there are two groups of people. There are those who are strong in faith and those who are weak in faith. We might tend to think that the person who is strong in his faith is the person who works hard to avoid any behavior that might be spiritually suspicious. The person with strong faith, we think, is probably the person with the longer "do not" list.

But Romans 14 paints the opposite picture. The "strong in faith" person is described as someone who has liberty of conscience in the gray areas of life. The "weak in faith" person is described as someone who more scrupulously regulates his or her behavior.

When it comes to matters of conscience, if someone exercises liberty in an area where your conscience will not allow you to do the same, do you judge that person as less committed or less holy or less devoted to Jesus than you are?

If so, you are weak in your faith. Why? Because you believe that having a longer "do not" list will somehow earn you greater favor with God. You're thinking that even though God hasn't put a particular activity off limits for his children, your high moral standards in these gray areas should count for something with God. You begin to think that your standards are the proper moral standards, and that everyone would be better off if they'd choose to live as you are choosing to live.

But what about when someone takes a verse like "your body is a temple of the Holy Spirit" (1 Cor. 6:19) and then tries to tell you that as a Christian it's wrong to eat GMO foods? Or that if you don't take the right kinds of supplements you're not caring for your temple the way you should? Or that if you don't go to the gym as often as they do, you aren't taking your faith seriously enough?

Let's say your husband grew up chewing tobacco. And he knows you think it's gross. And he's agreed not to do it when you're around. But you know he still chews and you think it's gross. You've showed him the pictures of the people who had cancer of the jaw from chewing. You've told him you really wish he'd quit. But you can see that he has a bag of Red Man in his back pocket sometimes. And it bugs you.

This is where a wife (or a husband, for that matter) can be tempted to play a spiritual trump card. You say things like, "I seriously doubt Jesus ever chewed tobacco." You Google "Bible verses about smoking" to find whatever ammo you can to try to guilt your husband into quitting.

When you do that, here's what you're doing. You're trying to turn a personal preference into a universal, nonnegotiable standard of righteousness. And people who do that, according to Romans 14, are people who are weak in faith.

Now let's be clear. All of us are called to apply biblical wisdom in our lives. The body *is* the temple of the Holy Spirit. That means something. That reality has implications for our choices. God calls us to steward our physical health. It's right and appropriate for us to challenge each other in these kinds of matters.

We also are called on by God to think carefully about the way our personal choices affect others. The apostle Paul says there were areas where he chose not to exercise liberty because of his love for others. Galatians 5:13 warns about our responsibility to put limits on how we exercise our freedom in Christ: "You were called to freedom, brothers. Only do not use your freedom as an opportunity for the flesh, but through love serve one another."

I have a friend who faced this issue when he became engaged. My friend had always enjoyed having a glass of wine with a meal. His fiancée had chosen not to drink any alcohol. As the couple talked about the issue, the bride-to-be, who recognized this as an area of Christian liberty, admitted that it would be hard for her to be married to a man who chose to drink.

How was the issue ultimately resolved? The husband-to-be chose to die to self and to serve his wife by agreeing that he would give up his glass of wine. He loved her more than he loved his freedom in this area.

There's clearly a balance here. Problems can come when we choose to flaunt our liberty in Christ without concern for or love for someone else, or when we attempt to turn matters of personal preference or personal application into biblical absolutes. When we attach the label of "wrongdoing" or sin to something the Bible does not clearly prohibit, we have skated over to the thin-ice part of the pond where the Pharisees congregate. At the same time, when we place a higher value on our liberty in Christ than we do on how our actions will affect someone else, we've lost sight of what it means to love someone else.

In either case, the instruction of Scripture is that we are not to continue to quarrel over these kinds of disputed matters. We are not to despise one another because we don't agree. We are not to pass judgment on one another for making different choices. John Stott wisely says, "The best way to determine what our attitude to other people should be is to determine what God's attitude to them is."[2] The problem is, some of us are just sure God shares our opinion about things!

If you're married to someone who exercises liberty in areas of preference or opinion, even if your conscience is troubled by their choice, you are not to pass judgment on them. Pointedly, the apostle Paul asks, "Who are you to pass judgment on the servant of another?" (Rom. 14:4a).

If you find yourself lapsing into judgmentalism toward your spouse, don't ignore the issue. Deal with it. First, humble yourself. Ask yourself, *Who am I to pass judgment on someone else?* Meditate on the gospel and reflect on what Jesus has done for you. While you were still a sinner, he didn't judge you. He died for you. His love was instrumental in your spiritual transformation.

And ask yourself if you have been guilty of any of these sins of omission when it comes to your spouse. Set aside your "do not" list for a minute and ask yourself about the "to do" list that God has given you.

> Have you served your spouse? (Gal. 5:13)
>
> Been kind to them? (Eph. 4:29)
>
> Cared for them? (1 Cor. 12:25)
>
> Helped with a burden? (Gal. 6:2)
>
> Encouraged them? (1 Thess. 5:11)
>
> Spurred them to good deeds? (Heb. 10:24)

Talk Together

1. Would you say your walk with Jesus is more character-ized by structure and discipline and order, or by flexibility and freedom? What are one or two dangers that might accompany your perpective?

2. Are there "disputed matters" that have been a source of conflict in your relationship? What does it look like to love someone well when we find ourselves on opposite sides of a "disputable matter?"

CHAPTER 8

The Truth, the Whole Truth, and Nothing But: Love Is Honest

Love rejoices with the truth.
(1 Cor. 13:6b)

*T*he American Film Institute loves making lists. On their website, you'll find lists of everything from the 100 best film scores to the 100 best movie heroes and villains. There's even a list for the top 100 most memorable lines from movies—phrases like "I've got a feeling we're not in Kansas anymore" that have taken on a life of their own and even inspired annual celebrations ("May the 4th be with you").

Screenwriters certainly have a sense when they're writing a movie script that a particular line will have dramatic impact. But there's no way to predict that a single line from a movie will somehow resonate so deeply with an audience that for years following the release of the film, people will still be saying things like, "There's no place like home," or, "I'm gonna make him an offer he can't refuse."

One of the movie lines that made the AFI top 100 list is from the 1992 film *A Few Good Men*. Anyone who has seen the film knows the moment near the end when Tom Cruise as Lt. Daniel Kaffee is cross-examining a superior officer, Colonel Nathan Jessup, played by Jack Nicholson. In a court martial hearing, Kaffee is pressing the colonel about the events that led to the death of a private under his command. As the questioning becomes more intense, Colonel Jessup looks at Kaffee and says, "You want answers?" Kaffee shouts back at him, "I want the truth!"

And that's when Colonel Jessup says the five words that are still repeated today. Words that came in at #29 on the AFI Top 100 Movie Quotes list.

"You can't handle the truth!"

I wonder if Colonel Jessup is right. I wonder how many married people just can't handle the truth.

What level of honesty or transparency is present in most marriages? How many of us recognize the link that exists between oneness and honesty, between genuine intimacy and truthfulness in marriage? And how many husbands and wives are falling short of the oneness God intends for us in marriage because we have thoughts or emotions or activities that we keep hidden from our spouse?

Can your marriage handle the truth? Love, the apostle Paul tells us, rejoices in the truth. But what exactly does that mean?

I think it means four things. First, I think it means that our love for one another ultimately flourishes in an environment where we are "naked and not ashamed" (Gen. 2:25).

Deep inside, all of us wrestle with insecurity. We are well acquainted with our own weaknesses and failings. We know that our public persona is a polished and manicured portrait, with the flaws and faults carefully concealed. We think to ourselves, *If anyone knew the real me there is no way they could love me.*

Then you get married and find that it's hard to keep your true self concealed when you live with someone. We long to be able to be honest and open with another person about our weaknesses, doubts, and shame without having to fear rejection. That's what being "naked and unashamed" is supposed to look like. It's what Adam and Eve had in the Garden of Eden before they rebelled against God.

Love rejoices when this kind of honesty and vulnerability can be present in marriage, without any fear of rejection. When there is nothing we feel like we need to keep concealed and hidden from each other. When we are fully known and fully loved.

Second, I think this verse is reminding us that there is a connection between love and trust. When we lie or mislead or do anything that sows seeds of distrust in our marriage, we are doing damage that can destroy the foundation of any relationship. Love rejoices in the truth because it's really hard to love someone we can't trust.

Third, I think the Bible is telling us that our love for one another will deepen and grow when we are committed as individuals and as a couple to growing in our understanding of the truth we find in Scripture. Jesus is the truth. Our love for one another will grow as together we grow in our knowledge and understanding of God's Word.

Finally, in the context of this passage, I think Paul wants us to be husbands and wives who are committed to aligning our lives, our choices, and our actions with the truth of God's

Word. As we've just seen, love does not rejoice in wrongdoing. Paul contrasts rejoicing in iniquity with rejoicing in truth. Love thrives when couples are committed to turning away from sin and making God's truth central to how they live.

Talk Together

1. Talk about a time when you were afraid to be honest because you weren't sure another person could handle it.

2. When was a time you shared a hard truth with someone? What was your motivation? How can remembering your motivation when you have shared hard truths with others help you receive it when they share hard truths with you?

When we marry, there is a hidden hope in our hearts. I don't think it's a conscious desire, but I think all of us are hoping that we might have actually found someone who knows us in spite of all our imperfections and idiosyncrasies. We are people who long to be fully known *and* fully loved.

But over the years, we've come to believe that there are some things about us—things we think or things we've done—that we need to keep locked away from anyone in order to be accepted and loved. Maybe we got up the nerve at some point to drop our guard and be honest with another person about who we really are, only to experience rejection. All of a sudden, the person we thought was a trusted friend starts to back away from us relationally. Or maybe our own sense of shame has convinced us that if someone knew "the real me" they couldn't possibly still love us. That shame leaves us convinced that we are unlovable.

And then it happens. We meet someone who seems to be attracted to us. Someone who wants to know us better, and who doesn't flinch when we carefully and cautiously begin to peel back just a few of the protective layers we've built around our lives. Hope starts to well up in us that maybe there is someone who would still find us worthy of love in spite of what we know is really true about who we are.

The great promise of Scripture is that this deep longing to be fully known and fully loved can be fulfilled—by God. The same God who has searched us and known us and who discerns our thoughts from afar (Ps. 139:1–4) has pledged his love to us and has promised to never leave us or forsake us. And somewhere deep inside every one of us is the hope that if God can really know us and still love us, maybe we can find someone in this life who can show us that same kind of unconditional acceptance and love.

Still, there's a voice at work in each of us that keeps whispering, *Don't let your guard down. If that person really knew who you are, there's no way he or she could love you.*

If we've read the Bible, we know where that voice comes from. The word in Hebrew that is translated "Satan" is a word that means "accuser." Revelation 12:10 describes Satan as accusing believers day and night before God. While he never quits making his accusations, God never fails to announce that, in

Christ, our sins have been paid for. We belong to him. We are his children. He loves us "with an everlasting love" (Jer. 31:3).

The way the Accuser works in our lives is through what are described by the apostle Paul as "fiery darts" (Eph. 6:16 KJV). The tactic he uses with God's children is to remind us of our failings and flaws. He regularly tempts us to believe that there is no way God can love us given our utter unworthiness. "There's no way God could love you," he whispers. "I mean, just look at what a mess you really are!"

Paul says that only "the shield of faith" can extinguish those darts. We fight fire with gospel fire. We preach the gospel to ourselves and remind ourselves of what is true.

God loves us with an unfailing, everlasting love. When it comes to how we are loved by our spouse though, there's a problem. Our spouse isn't God. He or she does not have the same divine ability to love us in spite of our weaknesses. God's grace is never ending. Our spouse's capacity for extending grace has limits.

That's why we often find ourselves functioning with a filter in marriage. We keep the worst parts of who we are—our failings, our sinful thoughts or actions—from one another because deep down, we're convinced that if our spouse knew us fully, there is no way he or she could really love us.

This is our subconscious strategy during the dating years. We make sure we present our best selves to one another. When we know we're going to be together, we make ourselves as attractive as possible. We put on our best behavior and work to be our most charming and most likeable. We don't want to do anything that might repel the person we are attracted to.

And when it comes to how we view the other person, we are prone to fill in the blank spaces—the parts about the other person we don't know—by assuming the best. By the time we're standing face-to-face, exchanging vows before God and witnesses, we've seen enough to believe that our lives together will be better than our lives apart would be. But it's all the things we don't know about each other, along with all the things about ourselves that we've kept hidden, that will begin to challenge our commitment as they become exposed in marriage.

And then our spouse learns something new about us—some shameful part of our past or about how we think or feel about certain issues—and he or she responds by pulling back or withdrawing. When that happens, we quickly get the message. Being fully known is not safe. We have to keep our disguise on and our guard up if we want to experience some level of acceptance and something close to real love.

Love rejoices in the truth. Love grows when we learn how to handle the truth about one another. Love thrives when we learn how to extend grace and receive grace in marriage. God's design for marriage is for two people to be real with each other, to be fully exposed and still loved, to be naked before each other, without shame. And that only happens when we start to grow as grace givers.

Talk Together

1. How can you show your spouse grace to ensure him or her that you love him or her unconditionally?

2. How can you develop a culture in marriage of openness and honesty?

Love will only flourish in an environment of trust. And trust takes time and care to build. But it can be destroyed in an instant.

It was a simple trip to the grocery store. My wife had given me a list and I had dutifully purchased every item.

Mary Ann and I have two different approaches when it comes to grocery shopping. She views the task the same way I think about a road trip. Her goal is to find the items she needs, check out quickly, and move on. But when I head to the grocery store, I'm more apt to take the scenic route. I like to explore. To go down all the aisles. There may be some new item, some amazing discovery awaiting me over on aisle seven. I might find a snack food that is calling out my name. A craving may emerge.

Since I was shopping alone on this particular trip to the store, I followed my preferred pattern. And sure enough, I came across a few items that looked appealing that were not on the list. One of the items was a bag of Cheetos. The moment I laid eyes on the bag of cheddar-flavored fried cornmeal, there was no turning back.

As I drove home, I began to imagine the disapproval that awaited me. I knew that showing up with a bag of contraband was not going to be looked upon favorably by my wife. At the same time, my salivary glands had already started kicking in. I could almost taste the salty cheesy goodness that was about to be mine.

I mapped out my plan. I immediately thought of the place in the garage where I could stash my illicit purchase before I arrived at the back door with the rest of the groceries. I figured that the items Mary Ann didn't know about wouldn't bother her. Win-win.

Cheetos were not the only purchase that was a deviation from the preapproved shopping list. But I knew my other impulse items—a bunch of green grapes and a few cans of soup—would qualify as acceptable additions to the shopping cart. Plus, they provided me with cover for the Cheetos. When Mary Ann asked me (as I knew she would), "Did you get anything else at the store?" I could own up to the grapes and the soup. Omitting the information about the Cheetos didn't qualify as lying. At least not technically.

This particular Cheetos caper occurred many years ago, at a time when grocery stores had just begun printing itemized receipts where they listed for you every product you purchased. My elaborate plan for hiding the Cheetos had failed to take this new grocery innovation into account.

Everything had gone according to plan. Cheetos had been stashed in their hiding place in the garage. When asked about any additional purchases, I had mentioned the grapes and the soup. It seemed like "mission accomplished"—until my wife pulled the receipt from one of the shopping bags.

"What about the Cheetos?" she asked.

Busted.

There is a reason why, in a court of law, witnesses swear to tell the truth, the whole truth, and nothing but the truth. I had told my wife the truth. But not the whole truth. And in the process, I had unwittingly sown very destructive seeds into our marriage. Hiding a bag of Cheetos may seem like no big deal, but when your spouse knows you're hiding something as trivial as junk food, she starts to wonder what else you might be hiding. In that moment, damage was done to the foundation of trust that is an essential component of any loving relationship.

Love rejoices in the truth. The whole truth. We've come to think of a lie as something that is clearly untrue. But our definition needs to be expanded. Any time we say something to another person and our intent is to somehow leave a wrong impression with that person, we've told a lie. When your intent is to deceive someone, you're bearing false witness. You're not telling the truth

A strong marriage is built on a foundation of trust. It's how we define our relationship with Jesus. We tell people we have put our trust in him as Savior and Lord. What underpins our relationship with him is our belief that God is trustworthy and true. We can depend on him. Jesus has declared himself to be not just the source of truth, but Truth itself (John 14:6). And we rejoice in him. We trust him. We rejoice in the truth.

Love and trust walk hand in hand. It's much easier to love someone who has proven himself or herself to be dependable and trustworthy. It's hard to continue loving someone whose word we cannot depend upon.

I've spent time with enough couples whose marriages have been rocked by infidelity to know that a single act of betrayal like that can take a long time, usually years, to repair. Trust is more fragile than most of us realize. We learn to trust one another over time. But that trust can vanish in an instant. And when it does, the only way it can be restored is through a process that involves humility, brokenness, confession of sin, the fruit of repentance, and the rebuilding of trust during a long season of demonstrating faithfulness and dependability.

While most marriages don't experience adultery and the trauma that comes from it, virtually every marriage experiences the subtle, Cheetos-hiding moments when we find ourselves shading the truth and, in turn, creating fissures in the foundation of trust that is essential to a loving marriage.

The Bible puts a priority on truth. One of the Ten Commandments prohibits "bearing false witness" (Exod. 20:16). The book of Proverbs tells us that our gracious and loving God hates, among other things, a lying tongue (6:17). In the New Testament, we're told to "put away falsehood" (Eph. 4:25). The apostle Paul makes it crystal clear when he says, "Do not lie to one another" (Col. 3:9).

I remember a conversation Dennis Rainey and I had a number of years ago on a *FamilyLife Today* radio interview with theologian Dr. Wayne Grudem about the importance of truth-telling. He noted, "In Titus 1, God is called 'the God who never lies,' or the 'unlying God.'" And he pointed out that in Hebrews 6 it says it's impossible for God to lie. So God's own character will not let him ever affirm a falsehood. "And that," he said, "is the pattern that we are to imitate. We are to become like him, and to never affirm something that is false."

Never? I decided to press the issue with a version of the age-old "does this dress make me look fat" question.

"So you're late to dinner with some friends," I asked him, "and your wife comes in, and says, 'How do I look?' And you look up at her, and you think, *Honestly? You don't look so great.* But you're in a hurry. So how would you respond to the question 'How do I look, honey?'"?

Dr. Grudem responded without hesitation. "I might say, 'Margaret, it's not the best. Do you have time to change it?' And we've done that. But, you see, now we have a thirty-five-year history where Margaret and I know we're going to tell the truth to each other, and I'm going to be honest with her, and she's going to be honest with me. Now, we want to speak the truth in love, we don't want to be harsh or unkind, but she depends on me to be truthful with her, and I depend on her in the same way."

Dr. Grudem continued, "Imagine for a minute—what would your family be like—husband and wife, parents and children—what would your family be like if you were sure that no one ever told a lie? What would it be like if you had a five-, ten-year history where you knew you could trust completely everything your wife said or everything your husband said—that there would be no lying in your family. . . . It would solve thousands of conflicts and thousands of problems, and the level of trust that would result from that would be phenomenal. It would revolutionize marriages. It would revolutionize families—just a commitment to telling the truth."[1]

The question for each of us in our marriage is: *How committed are we to being truth-tellers with one another, while always expressing the truth in love?*

We often avoid telling one another the truth because we're afraid the truth will hurt. Or we think, *That's none of your business.* Or we're trying to be polite.

My Cheetos caper was all about me wanting to conceal something I knew my wife wouldn't approve of or might be disappointed in me for. But a healthy, loving relationship can't grow when we always have to wonder if our spouse is telling us the truth. A commitment to truth-telling in marriage is part of how we love one another well and build a foundation of trust.

Talk Together

1. Are there specific facets of your life that you're really tempted to hide from others—particularly your spouse? Are they related to sin issues or just insecurities?

2. The Bible talks about the freeing power of exposing sin to the light, rather than hiding in the darkness. How can living a completely open and honest life with your spouse free you?

There is a stoplight we come to every Sunday on our way home from church. If you turn right, you can get to our house via a winding route that takes you through a residential neighborhood. The speed limit is lower than it is on the main street, but it's a lovely, peaceful drive with only two stop signs along the way.

If you stay on the main street and continue straight through the stoplight, you can travel at a higher speed. But you'll face three additional traffic lights and two stop signs before you arrive at the house.

The route along the main road is shorter. I've done my research here. Google Maps tells me it's 1.7 miles from the stoplight to my house using the main thoroughfare (which is their recommended route). If you take the residential roads, you'll travel a total of 2.5 miles. Google Maps doesn't even offer that route as an option.

If my wife is driving, she turns at the light. She takes the longer route. Her preferred itinerary is clearly, demonstrably slower (and therefore inferior!) to my regularly chosen route. She doesn't like the gauntlet of stoplights she faces along the main road.

I have demonstrated to her that the main road is the more efficient choice. There have been times when Mary Ann and I have, in separate vehicles, approached the intersection at the same time. She turns right while I press on ahead. And I always beat her home. Always! Still, to no avail. In spite of the evidence, she continues to persist with her flawed preference.

One of the key principles we learned early in our marriage is that different isn't necessarily wrong. It's just different. You might wonder why anyone in his right mind would choose a dip of Pralines and Cream over of a scoop of Deep Chocolate Peanut Butter. But it's a choice. It's different. But it's not wrong.

It's not unusual for husbands and wives to have different perspectives on a wide variety of issues. It would be odd if we didn't. As I've often heard Dennis Rainey say, "If both of you thought alike, one of you would be unnecessary."

The "different isn't necessarily wrong" principle has helped us cultivate humility in our marriage. We have ultimately benefitted from our dissimilar ways of thinking about things. But Mary Ann has also been quick to remind me that, on occasion, different is wrong. Not everything is a preference. Ice cream flavors are one thing. But truth is something else.

Love rejoices in truth, and one of the implications of that is that, as husbands and wives, we demonstrate our love for each other and for God by aligning our lives, individually and as a couple, around the truth of God's Word. Pursuing truth together—loving truth—and then making choices based on what God's Word reveals as true is a key part of how we love one another.

The apostle John wrote that in Jesus' incarnation, he put the glory of God on display for us. He was, John tells us, "full of grace and truth" (John 1:14).

Think about that for a minute. Jesus was (and is) 100-percent committed to giving us what we don't deserve and cannot earn for ourselves (grace). God's unmerited favor is on display every time a rebellious enemy responds to Christ's love and is welcomed into his family. John says God's love for us is like no kind of love we've ever seen before (1 John 3:1). Look at it, John says. Stare at it. Marvel at it.

At the same time, Jesus is 100-percent committed to truth. He is truth. He cannot be otherwise. To minimize or compromise on truth would be an act of cosmic treason. And it is as we believe and begin to align our lives with God's truth that we grow to be more like him. We are sanctified by believing and acting on truth (John 17:17).

Preferences are one thing. As we've already seen, love grows when we don't insist on our own way but give grace to one another in our preferences.

But when it comes to areas of faith and practice where God's Word is clear, love grows as husbands and wives commit themselves to knowing, believing, and responding to truth.

What that's meant in our marriage is that both of us have cheered one another on as we have dug deep into God's Word. For years, Mary Ann was involved with Bible Study Fellowship. Anyone who has ever done BSF knows that in addition to the weekly meetings, there is some serious homework involved. The regular discipline of going through the study notes each day and thinking carefully about what the text is teaching was a significant contribution to Mary Ann's understanding of Scripture.

There were times when her involvement with BSF meant that I had to watch the kids or take on additional responsibilities so she would have time to attend her weekly class or do her homework. But the benefits more than outweighed any burden. Seeing my wife grow spiritually was more than worth any imposition I might have experienced.

My own pattern for spiritual growth has always been different. My wife learns best in a setting that involves a routine and regimen. Maybe it's because of a lack of self-discipline, but my own trajectory has been less structured.

I remember the year I made a New Year's resolution that I would finally read through the Bible cover to cover. And I remember the day when that resolution went down in flames.

It was January 4.

Here's what happened. My reading on that day was Genesis 12–15. I'd pressed through the first 11 chapters of Genesis, with my mind buzzing as I read. I'd read about the creation of the world, about life in the Garden of Eden, about Adam and Eve's rebellion, about the first fratricide, about people living for hundreds of years, about Enoch walking with God until he was no more, about the Nephilim, about the ark, and the flood, and the Tower of Babel. All of that in only eleven chapters!

On January 4, I opened my Bible to the first verses of Genesis 12, where God establishes his covenant with Abram. That day I read about Abram's journey to Egypt where he lied to the Pharaoh and said that Sarai was his sister and not his wife. I read about Abram and his nephew Lot dividing the land God was giving them and separating from each other. I read about Abram rescuing his nephew after the enemy had taken him captive. I read about Abram being blessed by Melchizedek. I read about the night when God had Abram look at the stars and promised that he would have more descendants than there were stars in the sky. And I read about the ceremony where God sealed his promise with animal sacrifices.

My head was spinning. I had so many questions! This story was new to me, and there was so much to explore. I closed my Bible and made a new resolution that night. I was going to slow down and do a deep dive into the life of Abraham. I wanted answers to my questions!

So for the next four months, that's what I did. Armed with commentaries and books about the life of the great patriarch, I embarked on an extended study of Genesis 12–25.

My wife and I have employed different practices when it comes to growing in our knowledge and understanding of the Bible. The method isn't the issue. What matters is that we are both committed to pursuing a growing relationship with God by seeking to understand Scripture.

Our spiritual growth together as a couple has also not followed a prescribed pattern. I know couples who have made daily time together in God's Word and in prayer a regular marital discipline. That hasn't been the case for us. I could blame schedules or personality types or a failure of my leadership as a husband— any number of reasons. I know that the lack of consistent time together as a couple in God's Word has been a disappointment to my wife.

Still, God has honored the ways we have found to rejoice in truth together. At the top of that list would be our commitment to regular attendance and active involvement in a local church. That practice has been foundational to how we have kept ourselves and our family grounded in Christ.

Since before we were married, there has never been a question for Mary Ann and me about where we would be on a Sunday morning. Church attendance has never been an optional activity. We don't ask the question "Should we go to church this week, or should we sleep in?" Central to how we grow together in truth is by worshiping God together as part of a local church. That regular practice of having our spiritual wheels realigned every week has kept us pointed in the same spiritual direction as a couple.

I'm not talking here about simply showing up for a weekly worship service. I'm talking about active engagement as part of an extended church family. At our current church where I serve as a teaching pastor, we routinely come back to a definition of church involvement that we've borrowed from author Paul David Tripp. He says that a church is a community of people who are committed to "Christ-centered, grace-based, intentionally intrusive redemptive relationships."[2] Those kinds of relationships don't happen if all we do is show up for church one day a week. They happen as we do life together with other people who share our commitment to pursuing truth.

Many people are familiar with the instructions given to parents in Deuteronomy 6 regarding spiritual instruction and faith formation with our children. The organic process of having intentional spiritual conversations throughout the day is foundational to our job as moms and dads. The same happens in a marriage relationship as we interact with one another regularly about our walk with God or about things we're learning.

For example, in the past four days, Mary Ann and I took a road trip. During our eight hours on the road, we listened to four messages together. Three were focused on what the Bible teaches about aging and preparing for the last season of life. One was a sermon from 1 John. After each message, we had a chance to talk and process and think together about how we apply what we'd heard in our lives.

Since getting back home, we've had conversations about people we know who are facing personal and spiritual challenges. We've shared with each other articles or blog posts we've seen online that we found fruitful or interesting. And we've met with others from our church for a discussion about how we process what the Bible teaches regarding the end times.

In our stage of life as empty nesters, we have more and more margin for these kinds of conversations than we did during the parenting years. But even in those busy times, we found ourselves having regular conversations about God's Word and our lives that were sparked by our consistent rhythms of personal spiritual growth and active church involvement.

The point is, rejoicing in truth means we intentionally align ourselves as a couple around the truth found in God's Word. We understand the triangle principle—that the closer each of us get to God, the closer we are to one another. And getting close to God happens in part as we commit ourselves to his truth.

THE MARRIAGE TRIANGLE

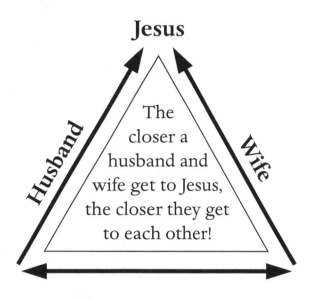

Jesus

The closer a husband and wife get to Jesus, the closer they get to each other!

Husband

Wife

Talk Together

1. What are your current rhythms and strategies for taking in the truth of God's Word?

2. What do your and your spouse's personalities tell you about how you should intentionally grow in truth together?

My parents did not have what I could describe as a loving marriage.

My dad was a veteran of World War II who was part of Operation Overlord, the D-Day invasion that was a turning point in the war. Although he never talked about his combat experiences, I have to believe he experienced what we know today as PTSD. In dad's day, they called it battle fatigue. Men who experienced the trauma of war maybe received a few days' rest and then went back to the front lines to continue to fight.

I don't know to what extent Dad's experience in the Army contributed to his decades-long drinking or his eventual diagnosis as "manic depressive"—what is today called bipolar disorder. But I know his drinking and his manic episodes had an impact on my parents' marriage.

In fact, when I came home from college in the middle of my sophomore year, my mom sat me down and told me she had decided to divorce my dad. She had clearly persevered in her marriage for the sake of my sisters and me. Now, with no children still at home, her motivation for staying married was gone.

I have never been a particularly emotional person. But when my mom told me she was getting a divorce, I began to cry. My tears took both her and me by surprise. "Why do you care?" she asked me. "You have your own life now."

"I don't know," I told her. "I just do."

I don't know what role my tears played in my mom ultimately changing her mind about getting a divorce, but she did. My dad's drinking and his manic behavior continued for more than a decade. But their marriage continued. Eventually, dad was diagnosed with malignant melanoma. By that time he was sober and attending AA meetings every day. They were able to have some good years together before he died in 1988. I was grateful that she was with him, caring for him up until his death.

I don't remember the context. But I remember a conversation I had with my mom while I was still in high school. Long before anyone was talking about love languages, mom told me that she found herself frustrated by the words of affection and the gifts my dad gave her. "I don't want to hear I love you," she said. "I want to see it. Don't tell me. Show me."

As we think about love rejoicing with truth, we can't forget that, in the end, the truth we're talking about needs to be a lived truth. It is ultimately not the truth that is being loved here. It is seeing the truth lived out in the lives of people that brings us joy. We rejoice as we see truth manifested in each other's lives.

Just as faith without works is dead, truth that is not lived out isn't really truth at all. The truth we say we believe has to be more than words or ideas. In the end, the choices we make and the way we live our lives are the truest reflection of what we genuinely believe.

The Bible contrasts "rejoicing in the truth" with "not rejoicing in wrongdoing" (1 Cor. 13:6). We've already seen that love does not celebrate or pursue unrighteousness. Instead, love celebrates and pursues holy, godly living.

The foundation for walking in righteousness is having the truth of God's Word working its way into every corner of our lives, where it affects the decisions we make, guiding, guarding, and governing us. We walk rightly—in righteousness—when we make choices according to how God says we should live instead of walking according to what seems to make sense to us.

Are you someone who walks in truth? When your instincts contradict what God says is true, which path do you take? When your boss says "do this" and God's Word says "don't," which choice do you make? When you think to yourself, *It's just a little sin and it won't hurt anyone else, and besides, it's probably not really wrong anyway,* do you listen to that voice, or do you run from it?

Proverbs says there is a way that seems right to a man—a way that seems to make more sense than what God says is the right way to go. We think that path leads to freedom, to satisfaction, to joy. But God says it leads to death.

Years ago, a popular Hollywood star had a major meltdown on the set of a film where he was the leading man. The audio of his profanity-laden diatribe was eventually leaked to the media and went viral online. The actor, whose job it is to play a part, was revealed as someone very different than the person we all saw on screen. He ultimately apologized for the outburst, saying he was out of order and his behavior was inexcusable. Still, fans who loved and admired his skill as an actor and the characters he portrayed were shocked by his behind-the-scenes behavior.

We have a word for someone whose public persona does not match his private behavior. We call that person a hypocrite. It's a word that literally means "to wear a mask." When a person says he or she affirms what Scripture teaches about godly living, and then chooses to live differently, the mask comes on. It looks good. It sounds good. But when the mask comes down and we see the person behind the mask, love takes a hit.

Of course, at one level, every one of us is a hypocrite. We can all relate to what the apostle Paul confessed in his letter to the Romans: "I do not understand my own actions. For I do not do what I want, but I do the very thing I hate. . . . I have the desire to do what is right, but not the ability to carry it out" (7:15, 18).

We've already seen how love rejoices when we can learn to be honest with each other about who we really are. The "naked and not ashamed" marriage where we are fully known, fully accepted, and fully loved is what each of us longs for.

But love rejoices when we see one another growing in godliness. Love rejoices when our lives line up with the truth we claim to embrace, the truth found in God's Word.

For love to flourish in marriage, we need to be husbands and wives who are continually working to see the character of Christ revealed in our lives. Love rejoices when we see each other becoming the people we say we long to be—people who reflect the image of Jesus in how we think, what we say, and how we act toward one another.

Love rejoices in the truth as we see it lived out in each other's lives.

Talk Together

1. Share with your spouse a few ways you have seen him or her live out the truth of the gospel.

2. If you are not yet married, what are some signs you can look for in a potential spouse that show that he or she is living out the truth?

CHAPTER 9

Be a Bulldog: Love Is Tenacious

Love bears, believes, hopes, and endures.
(1 Cor. 13:7)

*T*he call came unexpectedly, even if I wasn't completely stunned. It had been a while since I'd seen Steve and Christy in church, and I was wondering if there was something going on.

Steve and Christy had been married for almost a decade. They had one child and two busy careers. Both were bright, accomplished people who had been a key part of our church. So as their church attendance became spottier, my antenna was up.

Christy was calm when we talked, although she admitted that hadn't been the case earlier in the week. She told me that after weeks of denials, she had found text messages on Steve's phone that made it impossible for him to continue lying. He had finally admitted to the yearlong affair that Christy had suspected. Along with the adultery, Steve had begun using a variety of illegal drugs.

Christy had experienced a roller coaster of emotions since her suspicions had been confirmed. She told me that she wanted her old husband back. She was hoping they could find a way to put the pieces of their shattered marriage back together. She still loved Steve, but she was losing hope that their relationship could be salvaged.

When I met with Steve a few days later, I asked if he was ready to do what would be necessary to seek to reconcile with his wife and to begin the long process of rebuilding trust. He said, "Tell me what to do and I'll do it." I was hopeful. Steve didn't seem to be hiding anything and was willing to answer any question I asked him. He appeared ready to submit himself to godly counsel and accountability.

Three weeks later, Steve relapsed. And Christy said, "Enough."

When we read in 1 Corinthians 13 that love "bears all things, believes all things, hopes all things, endures all things," it's at times difficult to figure out how a verse like that should apply in a situation like the one Steve and Christy are facing. Where's the line between bearing all things and enabling someone's harmful and destructive behavior? Are we supposed to believe someone, even if that person has proven himself or herself to be untrustworthy? Should we keep hoping when we see no reason for hope? Is someone like Christy supposed to simply endure pain and betrayal?

What is real love supposed to look like?

There are no absolute answers to these kinds of questions. Every circumstance and situation has subtleties and context that should inform our decision-making. This is why God gives us church pastors and elders along with wise, godly friends. Hard questions like these require a lot of prayer and biblically anchored wisdom. We have to bring both truth and grace to the table as we deal with these kinds of issues.

But whatever decisions a person may make about how to proceed in the face of betrayal and hurt, we can't lose sight of what the Bible is saying to us here. Bearing, believing, hoping, and enduring need to be part of our journey. A true friend sticks closer than a brother (Prov. 18:24).

Love is tenacious. It fights to survive.

When we think about faithfulness in marriage, we think immediately of sexual fidelity. If someone asked you if you have been faithful to your spouse, you would presume they were asking about your sexual faithfulness.

But as these four characteristics of real love show, faithfulness in marriage goes much deeper. Faithfulness to another person means that when our spouse is carrying a burden, that burden becomes our burden too. Faithfulness means the default setting in our relationship is to stay committed to one another.

Mix tenacity together with faithfulness and you have a kind of love that refuses to give up on another person. When circumstances make it hard to love, as they sometimes do, a tenacious person digs in. He refuses to let go or to give up.

All of this grit and determination has to remain grounded in reality. The Bible is not saying that we should continue to blindly trust someone who has demonstrated that he or she is untrustworthy. Or that love means living in denial about what's happening in our relationship while we hang on to some kind of unrealistic fantasy.

But a loving spouse fights for his or her marriage. Winston Churchill once observed that the nose of a bulldog is slanted backwards so that the dog can continue to breathe while he hangs on to whatever he has his teeth sunk into. That's what a loving spouse is like. A bulldog. Someone who refuses to give up. Someone who says, "I'm here for you. I know we're facing some headwinds, but I believe the adversity we're facing can be overcome. And in the meantime, I'm not going anywhere."

Bible scholars say that the word translated "all things"—the Greek word *panta*—is better translated "always." Love always bears, always believes, always hopes, and always endures.

There are really two main ideas wrapped up in the four words the Bible uses in verse 7 to describe love. The apostle Paul uses a common Hebrew literary form called a chiasm. The first and the last words on his list of four fit together, and the second and third words belong together as well. We could group the words this way—love bears and endures, and love believes and hopes. Love is strong in the face of adversity, and love remains positive and optimistic even when things are dark.

Talk Together

1. What are some hard things you've had to bear during your marriage?

2. If you are not yet married, know this: it won't always be easy. How can you be preparing yourself now to maintain hope and belief during the hard seasons of life in general, or a potential future marriage in particular?

There is a term we use for people who believe all things. We call them gullible. And there's a name we use for a person who is always hopeful. We call them a Pollyanna. In both cases, we are thinking of people who are really sweet and kind, but who are naïve and probably not as connected to reality as they ought to be.

In the summer of 1975, I took a two-day bus trip with a group of about eighty high school students from Tulsa, Oklahoma, to Vancouver, British Columbia. We were on our way to a week at a Young Life camp called Malibu.

Two days of continuous bus travel is not for the faint of heart, even when you're a teenager. This was long before Wi-Fi or on-bus movies. We passed the miles by reading or talking to friends. But after the first twenty-four hours, each mile started to feel longer than the previous one.

Somewhere on I-80 in the middle of South Dakota, we found ourselves between two fields of cultivated farmland where some kind of plants with white blossoms were growing. Vicki, the high school senior seated across the aisle from me, looked out the window at the acres of crops and said, "I wonder what that is."

I'm not sure where the impulse came from (I blame sleep depravation and bus fumes), but with no trace of anything but absolute seriousness, I replied, "That's wild dental floss."

Vicki was not easily taken in. She rolled her eyes as she said, "Nuh-uh."

I did not flinch. "South Dakota is the leading producer of wild dental floss," I told her. "Where do you think dental floss comes from? It has to come from somewhere."

Vicki looked at me, and took a long look out the window again. Then she looked back at me. Still skeptical, but less sure of herself this time, she said again, "Nuh-uh."

"It looks a lot different before they process it," I assured her. "But that's the raw stuff there."

I maintained my straight face until she finally looked at me, looked out the window again, and said, "Wow. Cool."

Sweet, trusting, gullible Vicki. I started to feel sorry for her when, at the next rest stop, she was asking her friends, "Did you guys see the wild dental floss plants back there?"

When the Bible tells us that loving others means we "always believe," it is not commending naiveté. It's not saying we should trust anyone and everyone, even when our better judgment tells us otherwise. The Scriptures call us to wisdom and discernment. To simply accept whatever we're told would contradict Jesus' instructions to "be wise as serpents and innocent as doves" (Matt. 10:16).

But think for a minute. What is the mistake a gullible person makes? He or she trusts others too easily. That's what little children are like, right? They easily trust others because they are guileless. They default to believing the best about others.

What kind of faith did Jesus say we are to have? The faith of a little child.

We give another person a great gift when we say, "I'm going to put myself at risk and choose to trust you until it becomes clear you can't be trusted." I remember the phrase I heard theologian R. C. Sproul use to describe this kind of trust. He called it giving "the judgment of charity." It's more commonly referred to as giving someone the benefit of the doubt.

Though it's not used as much today, the term Pollyanna used to refer to someone who chooses to believe the best about another person and to remain hopeful in the face of adversity. It's all due to the eponymously titled classic children's book written by Eleanor Porter in 1913 and then turned into a movie by Walt Disney in 1960. Because of the book and the movie, people came to think of anyone who was always optimistic and unflaggingly hopeful as a Pollyanna.

The movie tells the story of an orphan who comes to live with her rich, lonely Aunt Polly, who has lived an isolated life because she has loved and been hurt before. All of a sudden, into her life comes her always cheerful and positive niece.

In one scene in the movie, Pollyanna goes to see Mrs. Snow, a wealthy but lonely hypochondriac. When Pollyanna arrives, Mrs. Snow is meeting with the undertaker to select the fabric for her coffin. (She's not sick, or even ailing in any way, but she's always reminding her friends that she could die at any moment.) Pollyanna tells Mrs. Snow about how her father, a minister, taught her to play "the glad game" when she was a child. Pollyanna explains that when she was a little girl she wanted a doll, but her family was too poor to buy her one. So her father asked the people at the missionary society if they might be able to send his daughter a secondhand doll. But there was some kind of mix-up, and instead of a doll, the family received a pair of crutches.

In the face of her disappointment, Pollyanna's father said the whole family should play "the glad game" and find something to be glad about. Pollyanna explains to Mrs. Snow that after she played the glad game for a while, she found she wasn't sad about not having a doll anymore. She was glad that she didn't need the crutches.

Today, if we call someone a Pollyanna, it's often a disparaging term. A follower of Jesus ought not be blindly optimistic. But he or she should be confident even in the midst of hard circumstances, because of a bedrock belief in the goodness of God. "In any and every circumstance," the apostle Paul wrote, "I have learned the secret of facing plenty and hunger, abundance and need" (Phil. 4:12). Contentment in every circumstance comes when we understand and learn how to trust in the providence of a good and loving God. Only then can we say with Paul, "I can do all things through him who strengthens me" (v. 13).

Long before author Ann Voskamp started making lists of the blessings in her daily life—lists that eventually became a bestselling book called *A Thousand Blessings*—Pollyanna had already learned the power of believing and hoping. "When you're hunting for the glad things," she says in the movie, "you sort of forget the other kind."

One writer says "love always believes" means "agape always takes the kindest view."[1] It takes God at his word and people at face value. It is eager to believe the best about others in a world that is always ready to believe the worst about people.

Pollyanna always believed. She never lost hope. She never gave up.

Choosing to trust and remain hopeful is a gift of love we give someone else. Think about that for a minute. If we call a perpetually optimistic and hopeful person a Pollyanna, what do we call a person who doesn't believe anything? A skeptic. A doubter.

A cynic. Cynicism, skepticism, and doubt are not attitudes we associate with love.

If the name Pollyanna doesn't ring a bell with you, maybe the names Statler and Waldorf do. Statler and Waldorf are the names of two of Jim Henson's Muppets who would sit in the balcony and talk about how bad everything was whenever the other Muppets were putting on a show.

If you had to spend the day with either Pollyanna or Statler and Waldorf, whom would you pick? After you'd spent the whole day together, either with Pollyanna trying to cheer you up and putting the best spin on whatever happened, or with the two grouches grousing about everything and everyone, at the end of that day, who do you think you would say was the more loving person?

A cynic is not a lover. A person who doubts is not a lover. Neither is a skeptic. The cynic might say, "I'm just being a realist here." But the truth is, cynics are predisposed to question motives and wonder about the judgment of others. They default to believing the worst. Or if not the worst, certainly not the best.

Talk Together

1. Are you prone toward blind optimism or cynical pessimism? What might be some steps to take toward the hopeful, honest optimism of the Bible?

2. Share with your spouse about a person in your life who is incredibly hopeful and optimistic. What do you like about that person? Do people like to spend time around him or her? Is the person a Christian?

In marriage, we desperately need the strength and support and hope that comes from a spouse who chooses to believe and who remains hopeful even in adversity. Each of us will have seasons of discouragement, doubt, and despair. In those seasons, we need our spouse to love us with hopeful, affirming words. We need someone who believes in us. Someone who will cheer us on.

Let's say you're headed to a college football game. Imagine for a minute that you're a bit discouraged because after your team won the first three games of the season, they went on a seven-game losing streak. If they lose this next game, it will be the longest losing streak in school history. And imagine the team they're playing is undefeated and ranked #1 in the nation.

It would not be unloving to say, "It's unlikely our team will win today's game." When the Bible says, "Love believes all things," it's not saying we should set aside the facts and cling to a foolish presumption that our underdog team is going to win against all odds.

But a loving backer of his or her favorite team will still cheer for and support the players as they come into the stadium. Throughout the game, that fan will encourage the players and exhort them to play hard. Winning may be unlikely, but it's not impossible.

Meanwhile, the guy who sits in the stands and says, "Well, let's see if this bunch of losers can at least keep from getting shut out," isn't the poster boy for the cheer squad, is he? He may say, "I'm just being realistic," but when frustration turns to cynicism and contempt, love has left the stadium.

At the core, when the Bible calls us to always believe and to always hope, it's calling us to something that goes deeper than simply cheering on a team or a spouse or a child, even when things are bad. When the apostle Paul says that love believes all things, he is not teaching us to put our absolute, unfailing faith in other people. He's telling us to put our absolute, unfailing faith in God and in his power to work in the lives of every human being. He's telling us that one of the ways we love others is by believing that God has the power to redeem flawed, failing human beings, and that he has the power to bring beauty from the ashes of anyone's life.

In other words, always believing or always hoping doesn't happen because our spouse always gives us a reason to believe or hope. Our hope and faith are anchored in God's promises and power to redeem, to restore, and to make all things new.

Someone who is married to an unbeliever shows love to his or her spouse by believing that God can and will forgive them and make them new if they will repent and believe the gospel. We love an unbelieving spouse by continuing to believe and hope for their salvation throughout their lives, no matter how they are responding to the gospel today. We never give up on them.

If we're married to someone who knows and loves Jesus, we love them by believing God for them when their own faith is faint. We love them by reminding them of what is true, and supporting them and cheering them on when they are discouraged, disheartened, or disillusioned. We love them by really believing that the Holy Spirit is in them, convicting them of sin and shaping them to be more like Jesus. We remind them that God is with them.

You love your spouse when you keep pointing them to what God is able to do in any circumstance, even when your spouse has run out of hope.

Love never loses faith in God's power to redeem any person who still has breath. And love never loses faith in the character of God and the promises of God for his weak and weary children.

What are those promises? When your spouse is fainting, remind him or her of a few simple things:

- God is there. He hasn't left you. He hasn't forgotten you or abandoned you. He hasn't forsaken you.
- God knows what he's doing. He is all wise (omniscient). And he's in control (omnipotent). He knows more about all that is going on in your life than you do, and he has a purpose for what is going on in your life.
- God loves you. He is committed to your good. He cares deeply about the circumstances in your life. And he has promised to walk through every valley with you.

You love your spouse when you live out a life of faith in God whenever you are with them. It is an act of love to believe God for your spouse even when he or she finds it hard to believe him.

And love always hopes. I don't think the Bible is telling us that we love others by having some kind of head-in-the-clouds, dreamer orientation to life where we are always thinking our big break is just around the corner. That's not what the Bible means when it exhorts us to be full of hope.

Then what does it mean? The opposite of always hoping is despair. It's always thinking, *It may be bad now, but hang on—it'll probably get worse.* It's looking at a half-empty glass and thinking, *I'm sure there's a leak.* People who lack hope are the people who say, "In the center of every silver lining there's a cloud."

Ever since I first read them when I was in high school, I've been a fan of all seven of the books in The Chronicles of Narnia series by C. S. Lewis. I read them aloud to my children multiple times as they were growing up.

In the book *The Silver Chair*, C. S. Lewis introduces us to a character named Puddleglum. Gotta love the name, right? Puddle glum. Puddleglum is a Marsh-wiggle, and as Lewis tells us in the story, Marsh-wiggles are notoriously pessimistic.

According to Douglas Gresham, C. S. Lewis's grandson, Puddleglum was based on Lewis's gardener, Fred Paxford. Fred was, according to Gresham, "a simple and earthy man who might be called a cheerful, eternal pessimist." If someone said, "Good morning," to him, he might say, "Ah, looks like rain before lunch though if it doesn't snow or hail, that is."[2]

We are not loving each other well when either of us allows the spirit of Puddleglum to invade how we think about life or about our marriage. Loving people are hopeful people. We have a bright hope for tomorrow because we know the One who not only knows the future but who is the Author of the future.

The apostle Peter says that, as Christians, we have "a living hope" (1 Pet. 1:3). The writer of Hebrews calls it a better hope, and says we should "hold fast the confession of our hope without wavering, for he who promised is faithful" (7:19; 10:23).

Our hope is a sure hope because, like faith, it rests in the promises and the character of a trustworthy God.

And in the same way that we need to have faith for others when their faith is weak, we also need to be the kind of people who point others to hope when they've lost hope.

There's a reason why the virtuous woman described in Proverbs 31 can laugh at the days to come (v. 25) instead of worrying about them. It's because she knows that whatever the challenges or afflictions she will face in this life might be, they are light and momentary when we compare them to the "eternal weight of glory" that God has ahead for us (2 Cor. 4:17). And so we keep on believing. And we keep on hoping. Not just for our own soul's sake. But because when we do, we're loving those around us.

Talk Together

1. What is the difference in hope and naïve optimism?

2. How can dwelling on the gospel every single day reshape your perspective and make you more hopeful?

Always believing and always hoping are twin graces that are aspects of genuine love. Always bearing and always enduring are the grit.

These characteristics of authentic love bring us full circle. The Bible starts describing what real love looks like by pointing us to patience as a defining characteristic. Bearing and enduring are the stuff of patience. The shoe leather.

Yell County, Arkansas, is an hour west of where I live. It's home to four lakes that fishermen love. It's also home to fewer than twenty-five thousand people, most of whom raise chickens or pigs or cattle for a living.

The locals refer to Yell County Road 49 as Dale Bend Road. Back in 1930, the Vincennes Bridge Company of Indiana constructed a bridge across the Petit Jean River on Dale Bend Road, about three miles north of Ola, Arkansas. The weight limit on that bridge was listed at six tons, which was more than sufficient in 1930 for the twenty or so locals or fishermen who used the bridge each day.

But on January 30, 2019, a GPS device led a trucker carrying a load of chickens onto Dale Bend Road. Once that trucker made the turn onto the narrow road, he was committed. There was no place where he could turn his rig around.

So when this tractor-trailer carrying a load of chickens and weighing more than sixty-five thousand pounds—more than fifty-thousand pounds over the bridge's capacity—attempted to cross the Dale Bend Road bridge, the almost ninety-year-old bridge collapsed, leaving the rig partially submerged. The Petit Jean River is not that deep at the place where the bridge crosses it, so the driver was not injured in the collapse. Officials ultimately had to bring in a crane that could lift more than 250 tons to pull the eighteen-wheeler out of the river. The cost of replacing the collapsed bridge was estimated at about a million dollars.

I'm sure the men who designed and built the Dale Bend Road Bridge in Yell County, Arkansas, in 1930 could not have conceived of the existence of a motorized vehicle the size of a steam engine. The cars that existed when the bridge was built weighed less than a ton. They must have thought their six-ton bridge would be able to bear whatever vehicles needed to cross the river.

Those engineers were a lot like most young couples on their wedding day. When brides and grooms face one another and promise to bear and endure whatever comes their way—sickness or health, riches or poverty, the good or the bad—they usually have no real understanding of the kinds of challenges their marriage will face. Caught up in the passion and joy of romantic love, two people imagine that their affection for one another will be strong enough to carry their marriage through whatever will come their way.

Real life has a way of putting those promises to the test.

I've talked over the years to couples whose marriages have faced all kinds of challenges. I've spent time with those whose spouse quit going to church. I've talked to couples who had to learn how to love one another as they grieved the pain of a miscarriage or the death of a child. I've spent time with husbands and wives who faced a wide variety of personality-altering medical issues or physical challenges that turned a marriage from an ongoing romantic escapade to an endurance race. I've heard far too many stories of infidelity, of drug and alcohol issues, or of foolish financial decisions.

And honestly, I've found myself wondering as I've heard some of these stories whether my own love for my wife would be strong enough to bear and endure some of these things. How much could my own heart handle? What would it take for me to throw in the towel?

Over the years, I've come to realize that when I face difficulties or struggles in life or in my marriage, God, in that moment, gives me the grace I need to sustain me. I might look at what someone else is going through and wonder if I could bear up under that kind of stress. But when the moment comes in my own life, the grace I need to be able to bear the burden is there.

God gives the grace *for* the moment *in* the moment.

It's important that we understand what bearing and enduring is and what it is not. The Greek word that is translated *bear* in 1 Corinthians 13:7 is a word that can mean one of two things. It can mean "to withstand" or "to cover." Scholars are divided about which meaning Paul has in mind when he uses the word here. The first meaning would make the word somewhat redundant with the word Paul uses for *endure*. The word for endure is a military term that means "to sustain the assault of the enemy."[3] Love perseveres and bears the brunt of an attack without backing down.

It's unlikely that Paul is intending to repeat himself exactly when he talks about bearing all things. It makes more sense to think that Paul is saying that to bear all things means to keep silent in the face of adversity, to be slow to expose or disclose the wrongs or faults of another person.[4]

Love takes no delight in shaming or tearing down someone else. Instead, someone who loves another person will hold his or her tongue and not be quick to make public the faults or failings of a spouse. "Love," author Lewis Smedes says, "has a fine sense for when to keep its mouth shut."[5]

Puritan Jonathan Edwards summed up the idea of these verses this way: Love, he says, "will not fail, but will continue . . . Whatever assaults may be made upon it, yet it still remains and endures, and does not cease, but bears up, and bears onward with constancy and perseverance and patience, notwithstanding them all."[6]

At the same time, bearing and enduring does not mean we enable a spouse's sinful or destructive behavior. I've heard horror stories over the years from women who have told me that when they reported to their pastor or a church leader about abuse they were experiencing in their marriage, they were told to go home and "turn the other cheek" or to submit.

Let's be clear. That kind of counsel is not from God. It's demonic. We are never demonstrating love to someone by making it easier for another person to continue sinning. We can bear with someone without being the target for their sinful behavior.

I recently spoke with a wife who had attended church alone on a Sunday because her husband was hung over from the previous evening. It was clear to her friends who saw her at church that she was alone that morning. So the question was an obvious one: "Where's your husband?" She told the truth, but not the whole truth. "He's not feeling well," she said.

I understand that a wife might not want to tell a casual friend at church that her husband is at home because he's hung over. That could be pretty embarrassing for everyone. And I appreciate this wife's desire not to throw her husband under the bus or to slander him in some way. But this demonstrates the fine line we must walk when it comes to bearing sin and enabling sin. This wife has to exercise wisdom to know that she is not making it easier for her husband to continue in sin by covering up for him or trying to protect his image (or her own).

Bearing and enduring also doesn't mean that we are called by God to bear burdens in our marriage alone. In fact, God expects all of us as brothers and sisters in Christ to "bear one another's burdens" (Gal. 6:2). God has given us an extended family to come alongside us, to pray for us, and to help us shoulder the load we're facing, whether we're in a marriage where we have to bear the emotional weight of being married to a spouse who regularly displays patterns of behavior that are oppressive, destructive, or abusive, or we're enduring the kind of practical burdens that come in seasons of financial stress.

Too many people I know have bought into the "rugged individualism" mind-set. They think that letting other people know they have a need or that they are facing stresses in their lives will make them seem weak. But the truth is, we are all weak! We need to learn how to fight through the embarrassment we face and to admit that our marriage is less than perfect. Bringing our needs out into the open and getting others to help us bear the load is part of God's design for us. Love bears all things and endures all things—but that doesn't mean we bear or endure them alone.

We find the strength to bear and endure hardships as we walk closely with Jesus and his church. When the apostle Paul found himself weary and weakened by what he described as "a thorn in the flesh" (2 Cor. 12:7), God said to him, "You can bear it. You have the strength you need. My grace is sufficient for you. In your weakness, I am made strong. My power is perfected in your weakness" (v. 9 ff). Moreover, when the same apostle Paul wrote to the Christians in Galatia, he encouraged them to "carry each other's burdens" (Gal. 6:2 NIV). God will give us what we need to bear burdens as we take them to him and to his people.

Talk Together

1. What are some unexpected burdens you have had to bear in life or in marriage?

2. Is it easy or difficult for you to share your burdens with fellow Christians? How can you grow in this area?

Remember Christy and Steve, the couple at the beginning of this chapter? As soon as the elders in our church became aware of what was going on, they reached out to both of them. Christy was weary. Steve was unresponsive. Although she was emotionally wrung out, Christy was still willing to do what was needed to try to preserve her marriage. Steve vacillated and eventually became completely unresponsive.

For Christy, believing and hoping did not mean that she was supposed to trust everything Steve was telling her. He had proven himself untrustworthy. Believing and hoping did not mean that she needed to hold onto unrealistic expectations about what her future held.

Believing and hoping meant that in the midst of all that was happening in her life, Christy followed the example of Jesus. She kept entrusting herself "to him who judges justly" (1 Pet. 2:23).

She always believed that God could turn things around. She kept on believing that God could bring her husband back. And even in the midst of the kind of hurt and betrayal she had experienced, she refused to hold onto bitterness. She refused to return evil for evil. She continued to hope that by the end of the story, God would bring beauty from the ashes.

Christy bore the pain and the scars of betrayal. As she faced financial challenges and the hardships of not having her husband helping with the responsibilities of day-to-day parenting, she endured. And she leaned hard into the love and support that came from people in our church.

At first, Steve broke off his relationship with the other woman. But it was not a decisive break. Over time, he went back to her. He quit responding to anyone who reached out to him, including calls or texts from Christy.

And so as elders in their local church, we stood with Christy as she made the difficult and painful decision to file for divorce in order to protect herself and her daughter. Even as she filed, her prayer was that God might use the divorce to wake her husband up from his sinful stupor. For her, divorce was a tool, not a weapon. As she processed all the volatile emotions she was experiencing, she continued to have compassion and hope for her betrayer.

Steve and Christy's story is not over. The central message of the gospel is that God moves heaven and earth to bring beauty from ashes. The call of love is a call to remain faithful. The path of love is a path that never stops believing or hoping that God might work in any relationship to bring oneness and unity. And when the journey gets hard, love continues to endure. Love bears up under the weight.

CHAPTER 10

Filling Up and Pouring Out: Love Never Fails

Love never fails.
(1 Cor. 13:8 NIV)

*I*n March of 1842 in Glasgow, Scotland, George and Jane Matheson gave birth to their first child, a son. They decided to name the boy after his father.

Young George Jr. was a bright boy, but his studies were hampered by poor vision. At fifteen, he began his course of studies at Glasgow University. He studied the classics, as well as logic and philosophy. He also wrote two books on theology. Clearly gifted, George started making plans to continue studying theology once he had earned his master's degree.

There are reports that during this time, George was also making plans to be married. He had fallen in love with a young woman. He had proposed and she had accepted, and the two were beginning to plan for their life together as husband and wife.

But George's eyesight was not getting better. By the time he was twenty, he was virtually blind. Doctors told him there was nothing they could do to preserve his sight.

When George shared his prognosis with his fiancée, she told him she could not face going through life as the wife of a blind man. She broke off the engagement.

Heartbroken, George pressed on in his theological studies, aided by one of his sisters who agreed to care for him. His sister had to learn Latin, Greek, and Hebrew so that she could help her brother master the languages.

Four years later, George was licensed to preach in the Presbyterian Church in Scotland. He served as an assistant pastor in Glasgow for two years, and then moved to a church in Innellan on the Argyll Coast of Scotland, where he remained for eighteen years.

It is said that George memorized his sermons as well as the hymns and the biblical texts for each service. Many in his congregation of fifteen hundred people who heard him preach had no idea he could not see.

In 1879, the University of Edinburgh conferred on him an honorary Doctor of Ministry degree. Queen Victoria invited him to preach at Balmoral Castle. She had the sermon he preached from the book of Job published. In all, George authored twenty-five books during his ministry.

In 1886, he took a church in Edinburgh where he served as pastor for thirteen years. He died at age sixty-four.

George never married. His ministry was his consuming passion. And given the challenges he faced as a result of his blindness, the fact that he had such a prolific preaching ministry is remarkable.

George Matheson is best remembered in our day not for his books or his sermons, some of which are still available, but for a hymn text he wrote.

George was forty years old when the sister who had been his caretaker for so many years fell in love and became engaged to be married.

Dane Ortland writes:

> The evening before the wedding, George's whole family had left to get ready for the next day's celebration. He was alone and facing the prospect of living the rest of his life without the one person who had come through for him. On top of this, he was doubtless reflecting on his own aborted wedding day twenty years earlier. It is not hard to imagine the fresh waves of grief washing over him that night.[1]

In an instant that evening, George Matheson wrote "O Love That Will Not Let Me Go," the hymn for which he is best known today. He later wrote of the text, "It was the quickest bit of work I ever did in my life. I had the impression of having it dictated to me by some inward voice rather than of working it out myself. I am quite sure," he later wrote, "that the whole work was completed in five minutes, and equally sure that it never received at my hands any retouching or correction. I have no natural gift of rhythm. All the other verses I have ever written are manufactured articles; this came like a dayspring from on high."

Here is what George Matheson wrote:

O Love that will not let me go,
I rest my weary soul in thee;
I give thee back the life I owe,
That in thine ocean depths its flow
May richer, fuller be.

O light that followest all my way,
I yield my flickering torch to thee;
My heart restores its borrowed ray,
That in thy sunshine's blaze its day
May brighter, fairer be.

O Joy that seekest me through pain,
I cannot close my heart to thee;
I trace the rainbow through the rain,
And feel the promise is not vain,
That morn shall tearless be.

O Cross that liftest up my head,
I dare not ask to fly from thee;
I lay in dust life's glory dead,
And from the ground there blossoms red
Life that shall endless be.[2]

There was only one truth that brought comfort to a blind pastor facing a dark night of the soul: he knew God's love would not fail. He knew it would not let him go. And in that truth, he found the peace his soul needed to continue with the work to which God had called him.

In our day, songwriters are more straightforward in pro-
claiming the steadfast love of the Lord for his children. Today
we sing about how God's love "never fails, it never gives up, it
never runs out."

After describing for us what love is and what it isn't, this is
the summary declaration found in Scripture. Love is endless. It
never falls down. It never falters. It never fails.

I live in Arkansas, where two days after Christmas in the
year 2000, we had an ice storm that left three hundred thousand
people without power. Perhaps the only good news about that
storm was that people who had bought emergency generators for
Y2K (remember Y2K . . . the disaster that never happened?)—
finally had a chance to use their generators!

Spending evenings by candlelight is only romantic for so
long, especially when you have children to take care of. And
it got cold at our house. In the middle of that power outage, I
found my supply of love was running low too. I was becoming
impatient. I was irritable. I was envious of others who had power.
I wasn't particularly concerned about my friends or neighbors
who were without power. I just wanted mine back on!

In the hours we were without power, I found myself starting
to think about life 150 years ago. How did people live without
electricity? We've come to depend on it. We trust that when we
plug in our fridge or turn on the light switch, the power will be
there. We build our lives around it. We expect it will never fail.
And when it does, we're not happy.

I was without power for a couple of days, and my joy was dwindling. How did our ancestors survive without light switches and electric ovens?

Real love never has an outage. There is never an interruption in service. Never a flicker, even in a thunderstorm.

Does that sound like God? It does, right? His love never has an outage. It never fails. It never gives up. It never runs out.

Does that sound like you? Does your love for others ever run out? Have you ever given up on your spouse? Have you ever said, "This far, but no farther"?

God's love is different than ours. That's what the writers of the Old Testament repeated, over and over again.

Lamentations 3:22–23 says:

> The steadfast love of the LORD never ceases;
>> his mercies never come to an end;
> they are new every morning;
>> great is your faithfulness.

Back in 1989, the Doyle, Dane and Bernbach Advertising agency in Chicago created an advertising campaign for Eveready Batteries. The folks at Eveready were upset that the Duracell people were claiming that their batteries lasted longer. They were miffed because the copper-top people were comparing the life span of their new alkaline batteries with older carbon-zinc batteries.

So the Eveready folks decided to fight back. They wanted to make sure people knew that their alkaline Energizer batteries would last just as long as a Duracell. That's when the people at the ad agency created the now-famous Energizer Bunny—the bunny who keeps going and going and going . . .

But guess what. In spite of what the ads claimed, Energizer batteries do eventually run out. They die like all batteries do. They last only so long, and then they give up.

Real love is different. It really does keep going and going and going. It never gives up.

Talk Together

1. How does dwelling on the never-ending love of God for you make you feel? How could truly grasping this love reshape the way you love others, especially your spouse?

2. How would it make you feel to know that your spouse's love for you was never-ending?

God's love for us never fails. When we are adopted into the family of God, we are never without his love. Isn't that what the Bible tells us in Romans 8? "For I am sure that neither death nor life, nor angels nor rulers, nor things present nor things to come, nor powers, nor height nor depth, nor anything else in all creation, will be able to separate us from the love of God in Christ Jesus our Lord" (vv. 38–39).

His love for us never ends. Never quits. Never fails. His steadfast love endures forever.

But what about our love for him? Or our love for others? Does our love run out? Do we ever give up?

We do, don't we?

I wrote earlier in chapter 2 about Hector and Maria, the young couple I met with for premarital counseling. They were the couple that wrote out definitions of love in mostly emotional and romantic terms. The core problem with their understanding of love as an engaged couple was the absence of the essential "never gives up" foundation that is necessary to sustain love for a lifetime. Emotions bounce around. Romance ebbs and flows. But real love has two things at its core: an unshakable commitment to one another and a willingness to sacrifice.

Romance is nice, passion is fun, companionship makes it all easier, but at the end of the day, real love is about a commitment to one another and a willingness to die to self to serve each other.

That's what the wedding vows are all about. Do you take this woman to be your wife, to have and to hold until death parts you? What about when she gets sick? Or when you run out of money? Or when life gets hard? That's what all the "for better or worse" stuff is about. Life *will* get hard. Your love for each other will be challenged by a multitude of things. But real love doesn't give up.

Here's the biggest challenge we face as we seek to persevere in love for one another in our marriage. We don't have it in us to love each other the way we should. We don't have enough love inside of us for our love to never run out.

This may be the most important part of the book, so pay attention here.

You've probably never lived in a house where your water supply came from a cistern. Most of our homes are supplied with water from a municipal water source or from a well that supplies our home.

But there was a time when people used cisterns for their water supply. A cistern is a large water storage tank that is supplied by rainwater. When it rains, gutters direct the rainwater into the cistern. The water is then used for irrigation, or it is filtered and used in the home.

As long as there is enough rain, everything works fine. As long as the cistern is full, you can turn on the tap and water comes out. But when there's a drought, the cistern dries up. You turn on the tap and nothing's there.

I've heard people talk for years about how every human being has a cistern or a "love tank." When we're born, our parents and caregivers start pouring love into us. The more we are cared for and cuddled, the more ready and able we are as we grow to be able to dispense love to others from our cistern.

Of course the converse is true too. If we are not loved or cared for as we grow, we wind up with a deficit and are less well equipped to love others.

This is why, by God's common grace, there are many loving and kind and gracious people who don't know Jesus but who are able to dispense love to others. You may have heard the aphorism, "hurt people hurt people." Well, in the same way, loved people love people. They can draw on the supply of human love that has been poured into them. And as long as others keep making deposits into their cistern, they have a love reserve from which they can draw.

But the reality is, for every single person, the love tank will eventually by empty. The cistern will run dry. Not a single person has an unlimited reserve of love to give.

LOVE LIKE YOU MEAN IT

Here's the good news: when we are adopted into the family of God as a new creation in Christ (2 Cor. 5:17), we are given a new supply line to feed our cistern. This supply line pours a steady stream of love into us. As children of a God whose love is steadfast and unchanging, we now are recipients every day of an endless supply of inexhaustible love that is high and deep and wide and long (Eph. 3:18). Now, regardless of whether or not others have loved us well, we have a perfect Father who has demonstrated his love for us in Christ (Rom. 5:8) and who keeps pouring his love into us. Remember, the Bible says that "the steadfast love of the LORD never ceases" (Lam. 3:22).

So for a Christian, if our cistern is low, we have to ask ourselves what has crimped our supply line. Are we regularly meditating on and reminding ourselves of God's love for us? Are we resting in his love and finding our joy in the truth that we are his children and he is our loving Father? It's wonderful to receive love from other people, but for children of God, that is no longer our primary source of love. Your ability to love other people is no longer tied to how much love you've received from family or friends. The source of your love for others is now the love you receive from God.

So what do we do when we have a day where we have no love left for others? You've had days like that, right? There's nothing in the tank. It's run dry.

Think for a minute. Is your cistern empty because God ran out of love? No! His love never fails. Never runs out. You've run out of love because you've neglected going to your Supplier to get filled up. If your tank is dry, it's because you haven't gone to the Supplier and said, "I need you to fill me up." His supply is endless.

We get filled up with God's love for us when we gather each week with our brothers and sisters to worship, to hear God's Word preached, to pray, to confess, and to take Communion together. These are all means of grace that God uses to pour grace and love into our cistern so that our tank will be full.

But a once-a-week fill-up is not sufficient, especially when we're facing stressful situations or circumstances, or when our spouse is just being hard to love.

That's why we have to keep being filled all day, every day. As we learn how to walk in the Spirit (Gal. 5:16) and be filled with the Spirit (Eph. 5:18), God's love is poured into our hearts by the Spirit (Rom. 5:5). As God pours his love into us, that love now overflows from us to others.

So how do you fill up your cistern? You meditate regularly on the gospel—on what Jesus did for you at the cross. You read and memorize his Word. You meditate on it day and night. You pray. You worship him throughout your day. You spend time with others who love him. These are what Pastor David Mathis calls "habits of grace." They are what God uses to refill our empty cisterns.

I know there are times in your life when it seems like your cistern is clogged—when no matter how hard you try or how faithful you are to spiritual disciplines, you're still empty inside. There are desert seasons for every Christian, when it seems like we're going through the motions and the tank is still dry. I've been there.

In those seasons, we have to go back to the cross and reconsider the love of God poured out for us. We have to ask God to break our hearts and move us anew by what our Savior willingly endured so that we could be rescued from our sin.

When Jesus called us to remember him in the bread and in the wine, what did he want us to remember? His broken body and his shed blood, right? That's what the bread and wine symbolize. He wanted us to remember his death, because it is his supreme act of love for us. Remembering his death and resurrection should, over time, begin to unclog any hardness in our hearts and open us up to the Holy Spirit cistern so that once again we are able to receive his love for us. And as we are able to receive and know his love for us, we are able to be dispensers of that love to others.

Love never ends. Never fails. Never quits. His love supply never runs out.

But we have to recognize that God's love for us has a dual purpose. It's to bring us comfort and peace, yes, but it's also to supply us with the love we need so that we can be dispensers of his love to others. We need to come to him every day, over and over again, to be filled up with his love so that our cistern never runs out and we are able to love others with the love we've received from him.

There will be times when it will be hard to love and not quit. Sin—our sin and the sins of others against us—wears us down. Loving others who have sinned against us is supernatural.

Corrie ten Boom was someone who understood something about this kind of supernatural love. Corrie and her sister Betsie were both single women in their fifties who were living in

Amsterdam during World War II. Their family home became a hiding place for Jews who were being rounded up by the Nazi soldiers and shipped off to prison camps. When Corrie and her family were arrested and charged with the crime of offering refuge to the persecuted Jews, they were consigned to the same death camps where the Jews were being sent.

Corrie and Betsie spent ten months in three different camps, eventually being sent to the Ravensbruck Concentration Camp, a women's labor camp in northern Germany. There, using a Bible Corrie had smuggled in, the two sisters led worship services, even as they were experiencing regular abuse and degradation.

In December of 1944, Betsie's strength gave out. She died a week before Christmas. Fifteen days later, as a result of a clerical error, Corrie was released from Ravensbruck. That clerical error saved her life. In the first week of the new year, the other women in Corrie's age group in the camp were taken to the gas chamber where they were killed.

Following the end of World War II, Corrie began to write and to speak about her experiences, about God's love for his children, and about his call for us to forgive those who have sinned against us.

Two years after the war ended, Corrie was speaking at a church gathering in Munich. She had come to Germany from Holland to remind people that God forgives our sins. After she had finished speaking, she spotted in the audience a man whom she recognized—one of her guards from the Ravensbruck camp. And to her horror, this man was now coming forward to speak to her. He told Corrie that after the war, he had heard and believed the gospel, confessed his sins, and surrendered his life to Christ.

"How good it is to know that, as you say, all our sins are at the bottom of the sea!"

He paused, and then said, "I know that God has forgiven me for the cruel things I did there. But I would like to hear it from your lips as well. Fräulein. Will you forgive me?"

Looking back on that encounter, Corrie later wrote,

> I had to do it—I knew that. The message that God forgives has a prior condition: that we forgive those who have injured us. "If you do not forgive men their trespasses," Jesus says, "neither will your Father in heaven forgive your trespasses . . ."
>
> And still I stood there with the coldness clutching my heart.
>
> But forgiveness is not an emotion—I knew that too. Forgiveness is an act of the will, and the will can function regardless of the temperature of the heart. ". . . Help!" I prayed silently. "I can lift my hand. I can do that much. You supply the feeling."
>
> And so woodenly, mechanically, I thrust my hand into the one stretched out to me. And as I did, an incredible thing took place. The current started in my shoulder, raced down my arm, sprang into our joined hands. And then this healing warmth seemed to flood my whole being, bringing tears to my eyes.

"I forgive you, brother!" I cried. "With all my heart!"

For a long moment we grasped each other's hands, the former guard and the former prisoner. I had never known God's love so intensely, as I did then.[3]

Our love fails. God's love never fails. The only way we can love and forgive those who sin against us is by filling ourselves up with his love for us so that same love can overflow from us to others.

This, then, is the kind of gritty, self-sacrificing, faithful, committed, rugged love that God has called every one of us to demonstrate over and over again to our spouse. A love that never quits.

For more than four decades, Mary Ann and I have had our wedding invitation framed and hanging in our bedroom. At the bottom of the invitation is 1 John 4:19. It says, "We love because he first loved us."

Even before our marriage had begun, we knew that God would need to be the source of our love for one another. Our love for others is feeble, fickle, and frail. But God's love in us and through us to others is very different. It keeps going and going. It never gives up.

He is the source of our love. And his love never ends.

Notes

Chapter 1: Everything Minus Love = Nothing

1. https://en.wikipedia.org/wiki/Head_shop

2. J. I. Packer, *Knowing God* (Downers Grove, IL: InterVarsity Press, 1973), 124.

3. J. I. Packer, *Your Father Loves You* (Colorado Springs, CO: Harold Shaw, 1986), 9, 81–82.

4. https://www.christianitytoday.com/ct/1978/may-5/corner stone-must-i-really-love-myself.html

5. https://www.truthforlife.org/resources/sermon/the-church-in -the-mirror/

6. Philip Graham Ryken, *Loving the Way Jesus Loves* (Wheaton, IL: Crossway, 2012), 21.

7. https://www.tedturner.com/2012/09/the-first-man-of-phi-lanthropy-ted-turner/

8. "And Can It Be," lyrics by Charles Wesley, public domain.

Chapter 2: An Odd Place to Begin: Love Is Patient

1. Names in the book have been changed to protect the individuals' identities.

2. Spiros Zodhiates, *The Complete Word Study Dictionary: New Testament* (electronic ed.) (Chattanooga, TN: AMG Publishers, 2000).

3. Charles Hodge, *1 Corinthians* (Wheaton, IL: Crossway Books, 1995), 238.

4. All quotes from Ron and Jan are from a *FamilyLife Today* radio interview with them. https://www.familylife.com/podcast/family life-today/what-every-woman-needs-to-know/; https://www.family life.com/podcast/familylife-today/realizing-theres-a-problem/.

5. Ibid.

6. Philip Graham Ryken, *Loving the Way Jesus Loves* (Wheaton, IL: Crossway, 2012), 76, Kindle Edition.

7. John Sanderson, *The Fruit of the Spirit* (Phillipsburg, NJ: P&R, 1985).

8. This was shared in a small group that the author was leading.

9. *Farther Along* is an American Southern gospel song of disputed authorship. See https://secondhandsongs.com/work/4234.

Chapter 3: The Thing That Is Better Than Life Itself: Love Is Kind

1. E. B. White, *Charlotte's Web* (New York: Harper and Row 1952), 164.

2. Timothy J. Keller, *The Timothy Keller Sermon Archive* (New York City: Redeemer Presbyterian Church, 2013).

3. Alexander Strauch, *Leading with Love* (Littleton, CO: Lewis and Roth, 2006), 44.

4. Jerry Bridges, *The Practice of Godliness* (Colorado Springs, CO: Navpress, 1983), 190.

5. https://www.familylife.com/podcast/familylife-today/giving -thanks-in-difficult-places/

6. Bridges, *The Practice of Godliness*, 191.

7. Michael Card, *Inexpressible* (Downers Grove, IL: IVP Books, 2018), 43.

8. Louis Smedes, *Love within Limits: A Realist's View of 1 Corintians 13* (Grand Rapids, MI: Wm. B. Eerdmans, 1978), 12.

9. http://www.newadvent.org/fathers/220133.htm

10. William Jones, *Ecclesiastical History* Volume II (London: G. Wightman, Paternaster Row, 1838), 360.

11. C. S. Lewis, *Mere Christianity* (1952; repr., New York: Harper One, 2001), 131–32; https://www.dacc.edu/assets/pdfs/PCM/merechristianitylewis.pdf.

Chapter 4: It's Not All about Me: Love Is Humble

1. https://www.merriam-webster.com/dictionary/humblebrag

2. https://www.urbandictionary.com/define.php?term=Humble%20Brag

3. Philip Ryken, *Loving the Way Jesus Loves* (Wheaton, IL: Crossway, 2012), 94.

4. Quotation is from the FamilyLife Art of Marriage video series for couples, https://www.familylife.com/art-of-marriage/home/.

5. Told to author in conversation with Dennis Rainey.

6. https://www.apuritansmind.com/puritan-favorites/jonathan-edwards/sermons/charity-and-its-fruits-sermon-7/

7. R. Kent Hughes, *Philippians: The Fellowship of the Gospel* (Wheaton, IL: Crossway Books, 2007), 76.

8. https://www.fpcjackson.org/resource-library/sermons/series/fighting-for-joy-growing-in-humility-knowing-christ-and-the-peace-that-passes-understanding-a-study-of-philippians

9. "When I Survey the Wondrous Cross," lyrics by Isaac Watts, public domain.

Chapter 5: It's My Way or the Love Way: Love Is Generous

1. https://storyofsong.com/story/my-way/

2. https://en.wikipedia.org/wiki/My_Way

3. *The Art of Marriage* Video Event (FamilyLife, 2011), DVD format; https://www.familylife.com/art-of-marriage/home/?popup=disabled&gclid=EAIaIQobChMI6ZOQxLWI5wIVg8DACh1RfQW_EAAYASAAEgK3TfD_BwE

4. https://www.familylife.com/podcast/familylife-today/what-is-domestic-abuse/

5. https://www.familylife.com/podcast/familylife-today/liberating-submission-part-1/

6. https://www.familylife.com/podcast/familylife-today/liberating-submission-part-2/

7. Ibid.

8. Jonathan Edwards, *Charity and Its Fruits* (Lawton, OK: Trumpet Press, 2014), 106–8.

Chapter 6: Keep Calm and Keep Loving: Love Is Unflappable

1. Alexander Strauch, *Leading with Love* (Littleton, CO: Lewis and Roth, 2006), 59.

2. Philip Ryken, *Loving the Way Jesus Loves* (Wheaton, IL: Crossway, 2012), 95.

3. Alexander Balmain Bruce et al., *The Expositor's Greek New Testament* Vol. 1 (New York, NY: Dodd, Mead and Co., 1902), 816.

4. https://www.reviveourhearts.com/articles/hows-your-love-life/

5. Ibid.

6. https://www.psychologytoday.com/us/blog/the-forgiving-life/201703/why-resentment-lasts-and-how-defeat-it

7. https://forums.catholic.com/t/is-it-sin-to-be-rude/333305/4

Chapter 7: It's Never Right to Do What's Wrong: Love Is Virtuous

1. R. C. Sproul, *The Gospel of God: An Exposition of Romans* (Great Britain: Christian Focus Publications, 1994), 232.

2. John R. W. Stott, *The Message of Romans: God's Good News for the World* (Leicester, England; Downers Grove, IL: InterVarsity Press, 2001), 361.

Chapter 8: The Truth, the Whole Truth, and Nothing But: Love Is Honet

1. https://www.familylife.com/podcast/familylife-today/ telling-the-truth/

2. https://www.paultripp.com/your-walk-with-god-is-a -community-project

Chapter 9: Be a Bulldog: Love Is Tenacious

1. Stephen Davey, "Will True Love Please Stand Up," *Beyond Puppy Love* podcast (September 19, 2016); https://www.twr360.org /programs/view/id,569560.

2. http://journeymansfiles.blogspot.com/2014/04/65-years -through-wardrobe.html

3. Charles Hodge, *1 Corinthians* (Wheaton, IL: Crossway Books, 1995), 240.

4. James Moffatt, *The First Epistle of Paul to Corinthians* (London: Hodder & Stoughton, 1938).

5. Lewis B. Smedes, *Love within Limits: A Realist's View of 1 Corinthians 13* (Grand Rapids, MI: Eerdmans, 1978), 86.

6. Jonathan Edwards, *Charity and Its Fruits* (London: James Nisbit and Co., 1852), 286.

Chapter 10: *Filling Up and Pouring Out: Love Never Fails*

1. https://www.thegospelcoalition.org/blogs/justin-taylor/o-love-that-will-not-let-me-go/

2. https://web.archive.org/web/20100411075459/http://www.cyberhymnal.org/htm/o/l/oltwnlmg.htm

3. Excerpted from "I'm Still Learning to Forgive" by Corrie ten Boom. Reprinted by permission from *Guideposts* magazine. Copyright © 1972 by Guideposts Associates, Inc., Carmel, New York 10512. http://www.familylifeeducation.org/gilliland/procgroup/CorrieTenBoom.htm.

BECAUSE EVERY
FAMILY MATTERS

At FamilyLife, we believe a strong family changes its corner of the world. It alters you, your kids, your kids' kids—even your community.

So our events, resources, and radio programs aim to equip, energize, and tune your life, strengthening your most important relationships with God, spouse and kids. For over 40 years, we've seen time and again that families with God at their core are those where the rest of life falls into place. We're not talking a pain-free or perfect place. We're just talking about homes directed and electrified by the One who made them.

We realize your family and the challenges you grapple with every day are as unique as a fingerprint. But your individual home matters immensely. Lean on us, laugh with us, learn from us, grow closer to God with us.

Let's journey together at **FamilyLife.com**.

Bob Lepine is cohost of FamilyLife Today®, FamilyLife's nationally syndicated radio program. Join Bob and hosts, Dave & Ann Wilson, daily for fun, engaging conversations about what it takes to build stronger, healthier marriage and family relationships.

f @FamilyLifeMinistry   @FamilyLifeInsta   @FamilyLifeToday

FAMILYLIFE®
Help for today. Hope for tomorrow.
| A Cru Ministry |